I0749795

Bloom

in God's Promises

Daily Devotions to Walk a Consistent and Confident Pathway with Jesus

Bloom Daily Devotional Series
Book 3

Mary Rodman

Copyright © May 2021 by Mary Rodman

All rights reserved. No part of this book may be reproduced or used in any manner without written permission of the copyright owner except for the use of quotations in a book review.

For more information, go to www.MaryRodman.com

Cover design by: SelfPubBookCovers.com/ RLSather

Published by:

Legacy Lane Publishing
Weatherford, TX
www.LegacyLanePublishing.com

ISBN:

978-1-954800-01-4 (Paperback)

978-1-954800-00-7 (e-Book)

Table of Contents

Thank you gifts for you...

Download your free devotions at https://maryrodman.com/landers/book-bonuses-for-bloom-in-god-s-promises

- ***Recipes*** A collection of devotions from *Bloom Where You're Planted* and *Live Life in Full Bloom.*
- ***Names of God*** Devotions which focus on the different names and aspects of God.
- ***Blooming Crazy*** A sneak peek at the first book in the next devotional series. *Blooming Crazy Life* will help you grasp the irrepressible love of Christ.

My Gratitude

My journals for the *Bloom Daily Devotional Series* have a gratitude section at the top of the page. Why? Because gratitude is so important. Recognizing our thankfulness on a daily basis keeps us mentally charged with a positive attitude in life.

It can be a challenge to keep your chin up on those difficult days, but expressing gratitude for even the small blessings like a flower in bloom, will help tremendously.

You can express your gratitude in a number of ways. Your spoken or written words. Through personal contact, such as holding someone's hand or offering a hug for comfort. Expressing your daily thankfulness to God through prayer is life changing. We become humble servants when we appreciate His greatness.

I am thankful that God has given me…

The mountains. I am most relaxed when I am in the mountains, especially the great Rocky Mountains. I am awe struck by the splendor of His creation.

My grandchildren. They are pure joy to be around. They are constantly growing, changing, and learning. There are so many lessons we can all learn from children.

My husband. We celebrated 30 years of marriage last night. I am grateful for every day we have together.

My readers. Without you, what I love to do would be pointless. Without your feedback and encouragement, my words on a page would just be words, as they would not be impacting someone's life.

Those are just a few of my gratitude thoughts today. I pray the following devotions remind you to have a grateful attitude each day.

Serving Him Always…Mary

Dedication

He has shown you, O mortal, what is good.
And what does the Lord require of you?
To act justly and to love mercy
and to walk humbly with your God.
(Micah 6:8 NIV)

I am a simple country lady who God chose to be His servant. God speaks to me during sleepless nights, and throughout my busy days. During these special moments, God reminds me—*"The faithful love of the Lord never ends! His mercies never cease." (Laminations 3:22)*.

Christ's unending love, mercy, and grace have taught me *"to walk humbly with my God."* Whatever life tosses my way, I know God has a reason and a purpose. That is why those situations are converted to pages in a book.

I humbly dedicate this book to my Savior, Jesus Christ. The One who walks with me daily, especially when I am writing. All glory is His!

Foreword

The SIGN of a Good Friend

As I sat down to begin to write this Foreward, I was thinking, "How do I describe my relationship with Mary in a few words?" I sought the definition of *friend* in a dictionary and reviewed Scriptures that talk of friends. Then one morning, I sat down to put on my makeup and looked up to see a little sign that my sister had given me which said:

> SISTER (noun)
>
> 1. Someone who knows everything about you and loves you anyway.

BINGO! That is how I would describe Mary. She is someone who knows everything about me and loves me anyway. So, I am going to 'take a page in Mary's book' and write something based on an everyday event – seeing a little sign in a new way.

I have known Mary for over 30 years. We went to the same elementary school and high school but one of us (I won't say which) was a 'couple' years older so our paths did not cross. But when she married Jim, who is a good friend of my husband, our friendship began. The things we have done would take pages and pages if I mentioned them all. Our kids were in her 4-H club, we did a couple's Bible Study for several years, and went to Women of Faith conferences together. We even organized groups of women to attend those conferences. We have enjoyed going to concerts (we love our Reba) and I have enjoyed helping her host her book events/craft shows. But the thing we seem to enjoy most often is going out to dinner with our husbands and catching up on what is happening in our lives. And I know she is always just a phone call away. We have shared struggles and secrets; sorrows and joys; and prayer requests and praises.

Mary's love for the Lord and obedience to sharing that love resulted in the most significant event in my life. I am most grateful to Mary for an invitation to attend a "Walk to Emmaus" weekend. Mary had been on one of these weekends and told me she thought I would enjoy this spiritual renewal weekend. I trusted her so I packed my bags and let her drop me off at a local church to spend the weekend. I had no idea what to expect. It was during that weekend that I gave my life to Christ. In that moment, sitting alone in the darkened sanctuary listening to *Written in Red* being sung, Mary and I became sisters in Christ! My life was changed as a result of that weekend. I will be forever grateful that she brought me to the place that would bring me into a personal relationship with Jesus!

Looking back at that definition for sister, "Someone who knows everything about you and loves you anyway." I can certainly say that describes Mary. But there is One that truly knows everything about me. God even knows my deceitful, selfish heart and still sent his only Son to die on the cross for me.

> *But God demonstrates His own love toward us, in that while we were yet sinners, Christ died for us.*
> *(Romans 5:8 NASB)*

I pray that as you read this book you will see the love God has for you and will be encouraged in your faith. I thank God for all of His gifts and bringing Mary into my life is certainly one of them. He has blessed her with a great ability to see Him in all things. May we all learn to do the same. ~Lori Zimmerman

Introduction

Bloom: A flower, especially one cultivated for its beauty. When you *Bloom* with Christ, you become a child of God who is cultivated for your beauty.

In order for a flower to bloom, it must first grow. The nutrients in the soil provide the necessary elements to produce a flower. As a result, the flower produces a seed or a bulb, and the cycle continues.

As a Christian, we have a continuous cycle as well. We bloom and grow. (Did you notice that I reversed the order?) You can say bloom and grow or grow and bloom, because it is truly a continuous cycle. My goal as the author of this book, is for you to *Bloom in God's Promises.*

Yes, Christian growth is important, but I truly believe growth happens when you take action, or exhibit Christ-like qualities in your life. Expressing your faith to others is how you bloom. Therefore, the more you bloom, the more you grow.

Each step of faith becomes stronger, and your growth comes from your root system, Jesus Christ. How do you and I find the faith to bloom is the underlying question?

Reading God's Word is a great source of strength and full of His promises. When I need a boost of faith, I read *Hebrews 11.* This synopsis of great faith is filled with some of the promises which God accomplished.

More great promises can be found in the New Testament, such as *Matthew 28:20b. "And be sure of this:* ***I am with you always, even to the end of the age.****" (Emphasis added).* When God said, *"And be sure of this,"* God wanted you to pay close attention to the words which followed. He wanted you to understand His promise to always be with you!

My favorite promise from God is that of His grace and love. No matter what I do, whether right or wrong, He always loves me. Redemption is the greatest gift God gives His children. A gift so wonderful, and so free, that we cannot fathom His ability to forgive and love us unconditionally. A simple, "I'm so sorry Lord," puts us back into His good graces. As you read the devotions which follow, I pray you always remember the promises—Love, Grace and Redemption—found in His Word.

> *Then Christ will make his home in your hearts as you trust in him. Your roots will grow down into God's love and keep you strong. And may you have the power to understand, as all God's people should, how wide, how long, how high, and how deep his love is. May you experience the love of Christ, though it is too great to understand fully. Then you will be made complete with all the fullness of life and power that comes from God. (Ephesians 3:17-19)*

Back in the Saddle

After weeks, no months of editing, formatting, marketing, etc. I am back in the saddle. My saddle just happens to be my office chair and my reigns are my laptop computer. It feels so good to write again. Don't get me wrong, God has been with me every step of the way, but when it comes to my books, my favorite part is the writing. I get excited about sharing a story, doing the Bible research, and tying it all together for you.

In the midst of the publishing process, my publisher, Diane, asked me "What do you plan to do after this book is published?"

I was quick to reply, "Clean my house!" which happened to be a total disaster at the time.

We both had a chuckle as she rephrased her question. "What are your writing plans for the future?"

That simple question made me long to write more devotions. Maybe one day I will break out of the mold and try something different, but for now I am committed to book three of the *Bloom Devotional Book Series, Bloom in God's Promises.*

What brings you excitement when you serve the Lord? For me it is writing, but we all have different areas of service. Once you find your niche, you will shine, because Jesus is a part of your ministry.

Psalm 138:8 says, *"The Lord will work out his plans for my life—for your faithful love, O Lord, endures forever. Don't abandon me, for you made me."* If we believe the promises in this verse, we should not fear serving the Lord.

His Plans *Jeremiah 29:11* is probably the most quoted verse when it comes to God's plan for our lives. But what about *1 Corinthians 1:25? "This foolish plan of God is wiser than the* *wisest of human plans, and God's weakness is stronger than the greatest of human strength."*

This verse speaks volumes about the abilities of God versus our own weak humanness. We cannot begin to understand what our future holds, what plans to make, or what strength we need for the journey, but God does. We need to tap into His strength for the daily journey as well as the long trail.

Faithful Love There are countless verses like *Lamentations 3:22, "The faithful love of the Lord never ends! His mercies never cease."* God loves us without end. Once again, a concept that is hard for our earthly brains to comprehend. During difficult moments in life, you may struggle with how you feel about God, but He never stops loving you. When we understand His love to its fullest, our lives are changed forever. On the most difficult of days, we love Him because He loves us.

You Made Me The words of *Psalm 139* always resonate in my heart when I think of how God made each one of us. Perfect. Unique. Wonderful. Quirky. Beautiful. Passionate. Crazy. Don't hide behind a mask of insecurity. God made you! Magnificent, original, wild, lovable you. He not only made you, He made you with a purpose in mind.

Get back in the saddle and head down the trail of life! On your most difficult days, remember God has a plan for your life. When you feel unloved, stand on the promise of God's unending love for you. Are you lacking confidence because of your unusual personality or your capabilities? God made you exactly the way He wanted you to be, and with a purpose in life. Find your niche in Christian service and *Bloom* as you remember God's promises each day.

Suggested Scripture

- *Jeremiah 29:11*
- *Psalm 139*
- *Psalm 136:5*

Mary Magdalene

I often wonder what it would be like to speak directly with some of the great saints of the Bible. I would love to ask Peter how it felt to walk on water. For Paul I wonder what was the thorn in his flesh? Was it a physical ailment, mental struggle, or a spiritual battle? But of all the New Testament servants of Christ, Mary Magdalene is one who seems the most mysterious to me.

Not mysterious as in secretive. Mysterious because I want to know—where did she find the strength to do all she accomplished for Jesus? We are first introduced to Mary in the *Luke 8:1-3.*

> *Soon afterward Jesus began a tour of the nearby towns and villages, preaching and announcing the Good News about the Kingdom of God. He took his twelve disciples with him, along with some women who had been cured of evil spirits and diseases. Among them were Mary Magdalene, from whom he had cast out seven demons; Joanna, the wife of Chuza, Herod's business manager; Susanna; and many others who were contributing from their own resources to support Jesus and his disciples.*

We have no other background about Mary Magdalene, except that Jesus performed a great miracle in her life. What else is there to say? Christ obviously changed her life. Once Mary discovered her Savior, she was "all in" with a servant's heart. She became one of Jesus' followers and part of His road crew, so to speak. She worked behind the scenes, and provided financial support. Gratitude obviously flowed from her soul as she showed her love for Jesus.

I have no problem serving behind the scenes, and I enjoy showing others Christ's love. What I want to ask Mary is, "How did you do it? When others could not, how did you sit at the foot of the cross and watch Christ's crucifixion?" Where did Mary find the strength to do something so difficult? We all face difficult times and unpleasant circumstances, but this was gut wrenching!

During Christ's crucifixion, all of the disciples fled out of fear except John. John, Mary the mother of Jesus, and Mary Magdalene remained at the foot of the cross. Mary Magdalene's heart was so grateful, she could not leave her Savior. She didn't fear for her life, and scatter with the others. She stayed at the foot of the cross with a broken heart, as Jesus suffered that day.

How hard it had to be for her to witness the agony and pain Christ suffered! But her selfless, thankful, servant's heart kept her there, until the bitter end. Out of consideration for what Jesus had done for her, she never left her Savior. She never abandoned Him for even a second. She was there when Christ was nailed to the cross, and she was there when He cried out his final words, *"It is finished!"* This wonderful disciple of Christ was there when *"He bowed His head and released His spirit." (John 19:30).* Jesus' death on the cross was a painful, heart wrenching, gut twisting, moment for Mary Magdalene and those who watched.

Throughout Jesus' years of ministry, she watched Him perform miracle after miracle. He healed the lame. He walked on water. He turned the water into wine. He removed demons. Jesus even brought Lazarus back to life again. Plus, the seven demons Christ cast out of Mary! She had witnessed His greatness over and over again. Yet at this moment, His life on earth was over. Sadness was around them as Joseph of Arimathea removed Jesus' body from the cross and placed Him in the tomb. I cannot fathom the depth of Mary's strength on the day of crucifixion, or the three days which followed as she and others faced the unknown.

When I am weak, God provides for me. Was it that simple for Mary Magdalene? Did she possess a faith so deep, and a love so pure, we will never be able to comprehend it this side of heaven? All I know is that God has given us a wonderful example to follow in His servant Mary Magdalene.

The Open Tomb

After the crucifixion, the Jewish people which included Mary Magdalene, celebrated Passover. They mourned the loss of their Savior, but their minds raced with unanswered questions. The Savior of the world had been crucified, and they wanted to understand all that had happened.

Mary Magdalene was grief stricken, but she was also mission driven. Her faithfulness didn't end at the foot of the cross. As soon as the Jewish Passover ended, she rushed to the tomb at daybreak to anoint Jesus' body with the proper burial spices. As they approached, her and the other ladies worried about who would roll the large stone away from the tomb, but instead they found an open tomb.

> *Mary was standing outside the tomb crying, and as she wept, she stooped and looked in. She saw two white-robed angels, one sitting at the head and the other at the foot of the place where the body of Jesus had been lying. "Dear woman, why are you crying?" the angels asked her.*
> *"Because they have taken away my Lord," she replied, "and I don't know where they have put him."*
> *She turned to leave and saw someone standing there. It was Jesus, but she didn't recognize him. "Dear woman, why are you crying?" Jesus asked her. "Who are you looking for?"*
> *She thought he was the gardener. "Sir," she said, "if you have taken him away, tell me where you have put him, and I will go and get him." (John 20:11-15)*

Jesus Christ chose Mary to be the first witness of His resurrection. He spoke Mary's name and in that instant, she knew her Teacher, her Friend, her Savior was alive. He had risen from the dead!

Jesus didn't appear to the disciples first, He chose Mary Magdalene! He blessed her for her faithfulness and support. Mary started her ministry with a servant's heart. She was a behind-the-scenes worker for Jesus who gave of her time, and her resources.

She was free! Free from her demons, and free to serve. She walked a life of total freedom in Christ.

She was thankful. So thankful, she never left her Savior's side on crucifixion day. She was with Him to the bitter end.

Christ knew Mary was a servant, but what He loved the most was her servant's heart. He could have appeared to many faithful followers, but He chose Mary to be the first witness. When He looked at Mary, He didn't see the person she was with seven demons. He saw the person she had become.

I strive to be more like Mary Magdalene every day. I want my life to be a witness to the greatness of my Savior. I'm not sure I will ever understand how she was able to witness Jesus' crucifixion, but I do know that Christ blessed her on resurrection morning for all of her great works and faithfulness. What an honor to be chosen by God to be His first witness, and have the opportunity to spread the Good News to the disciples!

Whether we are the first witness or the last witness for Christ, it is a privilege and a responsibility to share the gospel. Allow the story of Mary Magdalene inspire you to tell the world, "He is risen!"

Oh Man!

It is the first day of a much-needed vacation. We were packed and ready to leave late afternoon. Our goal was to drive a few hours to shorten the next day's travel, which we did. We stopped for supper and were very disappointed in our meal. Dry pork chop for me and four chicken tenders for Jim which were so small they didn't total one chicken tender put together. The side dishes rated in the okay department, and overall dinner was a huge disappointment to us.

Following dinner Jim said, "After that meal I'm looking forward our hotel breakfast tomorrow."

While we were stopped, I located one of our favorite hotel chains for the night's stay. We put the address into the GPS and traveled the last few miles to our destination. Upon our arrival, it was not one of our favorite hotel chains. Although we were disappointed, we \ grabbed a room.

The door handle to the room didn't work properly and it took us about ten tries to get into our room. Jim finally got the right jiggle and pushed open the door. We chuckled and called it extra security, as no one was going to break in without waking us. The hotel room was mediocre. The room was obviously old, but the beds were decent. The space was limited, but it really didn't matter because we were only spending one night. The television was a hoot. The volume went up and down no matter what the station. We drifted off to sleep dreaming of that wonderful hotel breakfast we would have in the morning.

Yea…the wonderful hotel breakfast. It definitely was not everything we dreamed of, but they never are. I'm still not sure the eggs were truly eggs, as they had a very strange taste and texture. The English muffin with peanut butter was somewhat tasteless and Jim said the sausage tasted odd also.

As Jim drove down the ramp onto the freeway, we discussed how the remainder of vacation would obviously be better. We looked back toward our hotel and what did we see? Our favorite hotel chain right next door! Our GPS took us to the wrong hotel and neither of us saw a sign for the other hotel. Simultaneously we said, "Oh man!"

After it was all said and done, I was neutral about the evening meal and the hotel room. I wouldn't recommend either location, but I had food to eat and a decent night's sleep in spite of the miscellaneous issues. Just like the church of Laodicea, I was neither hot or cold about the situation.

> *"I know your deeds, that you are neither cold nor hot. I wish you were either one or the other! So, because you are lukewarm—neither hot nor cold—I am about to spit you out of my mouth." (Revelation 3:15-16 NIV)*

Jesus is speaking to the church of Laodicea in this scripture. The people were stuck in a neutral point of view. They didn't speak against Jesus, but they weren't singing praises to Him for all the riches and wealth they had either. Jesus very poignantly tells them that they were nothing without Him.

This letter written to the church of Laodicea is also written to us. We are nothing without Christ in our lives. Our riches, our jobs, our houses, even our mediocre hotel rooms are nothing without Him. Jesus ends this passage with these wonderful words, "*Here I am!*" What a wonderful invitation to all who will open their heart to a relationship with the King.

> *"Here I am! I stand at the door and knock. If anyone hears my voice and opens the door, I will come in and eat with that person, and they with me." (Revelation 3:20 NIV)*

Suggested Scripture

- *Revelation 3:14:22*

Day Two

I would love to say our lodging for day two of our vacation improved, but it didn't. We stayed at one of our top-rated hotel chains. We had no problem getting into the room this time, the beds again were mediocre, but that wasn't the problem either. It was the water faucet.

We had driven for hours and were ready to rest for the night. I brushed my teeth, and the faucet wouldn't turn off. Jim tried, and he couldn't shut the water off either. Actually, I think with every attempt to turn it off, the water ran more. I don't mean drip, drip, drip either. I'm talking a steady flow of water. It was late and we were tired, so we did not call maintenance. We just let the water run.

Little noises bother me, so it took me quite a while to fall asleep, but eventually I did. Around 3 AM we were both awake and all I could hear was water running. (If it had sounded like ocean waves, it might have been relaxing instead of irritating.) Jim in his ingenuity somehow wrapped a towel around the faucet to ease the noise and we fell asleep again.

Upon checkout, I was ready for that usual question, "How was your night's stay?"

In a very nice manner, I let her know that I didn't feel the room was up to the standards expected with the hotel chain and how I had to listen to water run all night.

Her reply? "Sorry."

I was appalled! You're sorry? No discount offered? No coupon toward another night's stay? I was shocked by her lack of concern about our situation. As I walked away I thought, "Why did you ask about my stay if you didn't really care?"

After ample time to vent and pout, Jim told me to let it go rather than dwelling on the situation and ruining our trip. At that point, I snapped out of it and quit complaining. Over the next couple of days, I realized I sounded like the Israelites. Complain, gripe, whine, and complain some more.

After Moses had rescued the Israelites from slavery they became an unruly mob of complainers. Moses took their complaints to the Lord and He graciously provided them with manna and quail each day. *(Exodus 16:11).* The Lord's instructions were to gather two quarts of manna daily for each person and extra for the Sabbath day.

> *So the people of Israel did as they were told. Some gathered a lot, some only a little. But when they measured it out, everyone had just enough. Those who gathered a lot had nothing left over, and those who gathered only a little had enough.* ***Each family had just what it needed.*** *(Exodus 16:17-18 Emphasis added)*

Each family had just what it needed. Boy did those words hit home. Yes, the faucet ran all night, but more importantly, all of our needs were met. I had water to brush my teeth. A roof over my head and a bed and pillow for my rest. All too often we are unhappy with our surroundings and we complain. Our time would be better spent recording our daily gratitude and thanking God for those unrecognized blessings in our lives. Like a bed and a pillow to sleep on at night.

The Cabin

While on vacation, we rented a cabin for a couple of nights. The location was great, tucked back against the mountain and secluded. There was a wraparound porch which I enjoyed each evening as I sat and read a book. When we returned from our travels one afternoon, we were even greeted by three deer in the horse corral behind the cabin. They were apparently accustomed to vehicles and people because our arrival didn't bother them in the least. The inside of the cabin was well equipped with cooking utensils, laundry facilities, and all the usual amenities of home.

What bothered us about the cabin were the decorations. It seemed to be over decorated. The décor was fitting, but there was no place for our "stuff." If there was a corner or a table, there was a knickknack tucked away, and in most cases two or three. We even chuckled when we found a moose statue on the bed post of our log headboard. I know decorating is a personal preference. What appeared as clutter to us would be beauty to someone else.

It is the same with God. What appears to be clutter in our lives, God sees as beauty. The sins of our past, our bad choices, ungodly decisions throughout our lives can clutter our minds and clutter our hearts making us feel unworthy.

The Israelites had a lot of clutter in their lives. They were the product of slavery. God freed them, but they still had a slavery mentality. As I mentioned in the previous devotional, they did a lot of whining and complaining. Far worse than their whining and complaining was their lack of commitment to follow God wholeheartedly.

While Moses was on Mount Sinai receiving the Ten Commandments, they persuaded Aaron to build them a Golden Calf to worship. *(Exodus 32:1-6).* They rebelled against Joshua and Caleb when they wanted to go conquer the Promised Land.

(Joshua 14:1-12). They would continuously repent, and then disobey God again. Rather than driving the people out of the Promised Land, they made treaties with them and allowed their altars to foreign gods stay in the land. As a result, the next generation of Israelites were soon worshiping Baal. *(Judges 2:1-4, 10-15).* The list could go on and on about the clutter in the hearts and the lives of the Israelites.

No matter the sins of the Israelites, their bad decisions, or their ungodly choices, God never gave up on them. Yes—God allowed them to be taken into exile, but more importantly, God rescued them.

> *This is what the Lord says: "You will be in Babylon for seventy years. But then I will come and do for you all the good things I have promised, and I will bring you home again. For I know the plans I have for you," says the Lord. "They are plans for good and not for disaster, to give you a future and a hope. In those days when you pray, I will listen. If you look for me wholeheartedly, you will find me. I will be found by you," says the Lord. "I will end your captivity and restore your fortunes. I will gather you out of the nations where I sent you and will bring you home again to your own land." (Jeremiah 29:10-14)*

Like the Israelites, God longs to end your captivity of the clutter in your life. He is patiently waiting for you to seek Him wholeheartedly. God's promises are timeless. Remember God's words, *"I have promised, and I will bring you home again."* Come to Him today and leave the clutter of your life behind knowing God has plans *"to give you a future and a hope."*

Journaling

Years ago, I had a small book I used as a journal, but only for the book of Psalms. If something was troubling me and I found peace in the Psalms, I would jot down the verses which spoke to me, add a short note about the situation along with the date. I had totally forgotten about the book, and it was a wonderful gift from God when I found it the other day.

Not only does journaling help you, it serves as a piece of your past. Your history with Jesus is written down providing insight to your faith journey. I will be the first to admit that I am more apt to journal on the bad days than the good ones. I'm not sure why, possibly to unload the stress of life. So sometimes a walk down memory lane isn't always a pleasant one. Regardless, it provides a path for me to see where I was, where I currently am, and help me plan for future growth.

Within the pages of this small journal book I found both good and bad memories intertwined with nuggets of wisdom from God. I also found memories of forgotten friendships.

When I saw Dawn's name appear on the pages, it was a flashback in time. I seldom run into my old friend. We worked together years ago and shared the same love and passion for Jesus. We had many talks about our faith, and always encouraged one another.

When I wrote the journal entry, Dawn's job was being eliminated. She was struggling with the thought of losing her job, and I was struggling with the thought of losing my sister in Christ at work.

I snapped a couple of pictures of the pages and sent them to Dawn. When she read the journal entries she said, "Wow! That's such a memory of tough, tough, times. Thank you sooooo much for sharing this with me. God has blessed us greatly over the years."

Those words say it all! Yes, it was a difficult time for both Dawn and myself, but in the end God blessed us beyond our wildest dreams.

Dawn and I both left our jobs with that company within a few years of one another. We each had a few bumps in the road, but landed with our feet on the ground. Without our faith in God, we would have stumbled much more along the way.

Having the ability to go back and read the old journal entries, was a great reminder of God's faithfulness in our lives. Years ago, when we needed it most, we were reminded that...

> *The Lord is close to the brokenhearted; he rescues those whose spirits are crushed. The righteous person faces many troubles, but the Lord comes to the rescue each time. (Psalm 34:18-19)*

And the second verse on those difficult days was...

> *The Lord watches over those who fear him, those who rely on his unfailing love. (Psalm 33:18)*

It is wonderful to reflect on the goodness of God by reading old journal entries. They serve as a reminder that His Word never changes. The scriptures from yesterday are still true today, and He holds our futures in His hands.

Following my first devotional book, *Bloom Where You're Planted*, it was suggested that I create matching journals. ***Bloom in God's Promises Journal*** is available only on my website, www.MaryRodman.com/Books. Purchase your copy today! There is ample space to record your thoughts about each devotion.

Time

I had a slight problem with time this week. I left the house around 10 AM to run errands. After my first stop, I noticed the clock in my car said 9:15. I was excited that I had left home earlier than I realized. My second stop was to visit Dad. After visiting for about forty-five minutes, Dad kept looking at his watch. He typically does this when he is about to miss something important at his assisted living facility. I checked the time on my phone and discovered it was 11:30 AM. (Thus, his urgency to move to the cafeteria for lunch.) I obviously had not visited for two hours, and realized that my car was not on daylight savings time. Extra time came and went, but my life continued on for the day.

Time—there are many different ways to look at it. Time can help you maintain a schedule, or wasted time may represent the lack of a schedule. Time can be the number on the clock, or a reflection of a moment which transpired. Time is a measurable period of how long it takes to complete a task. It can represent a span of years as you reminisce of the past, or a plan for the future. Time is even the tempo which music is played. There are days when time flies by like an upbeat song, and other days, time passes like a ballad. You get my point, there are many definitions, with both good and bad outcomes. However, time with God has long-lasting results.

How do you spend your time on a daily basis? Productive? Wasteful? Somewhere in the middle? God tells us there is a time for everything in *Ecclesiastes 3:1 – 8*. God often calls us to spend our time quietly before Him. It is in those quiet moments that God will often reveal Himself to us and fight our battles for us.

The Israelites had been slaves for over 400 years when Moses came to Pharaoh and demanded their freedom. After all of the plagues God brought upon Egypt, Pharaoh finally released the Israelites following the death of his son. God didn't lead them to the Promised Land via the shortest route, instead He led them through the wilderness toward the Red Sea. *(Exodus 14:17-18).* God had one more miracle to perform for His chosen people in the presence of the Egyptians, the parting of the Red Sea.

Pharaoh's heart once again was hardened and he and his army chased after the Israelites. As Pharaoh approached them, the Israelites began to panic and question Moses' leadership.

> *But Moses told the people, "Don't be afraid. Just* ***stand still*** *and watch the LORD rescue you today. The Egyptians you see today will never be seen again. The LORD himself will fight for you. Just stay calm."*
> *(Exodus 14:13-14 Emphasis added)*

Stand still—a moment in time. God told them: Do not panic. Do not complain to Moses. Do not fear Pharaoh. Just be silent, capture this moment in time and simply watch as I perform another miracle on your behalf.

I gained and lost an hour of my day, all in the same morning. Oh, how I wish I had that extra hour—to capture a moment in time or to spend extra time with God. There are many scriptures where God calls us to spend quiet time with Him, but how often do we actually heed His Word and do so?

Suggested Scripture

- *Psalm 4:4*
- *Psalm 46:10*
- *Psalm 27:14*
- *Ecclesiastes 3:1 – 8*
- *Exodus 14*

Bloom in the Weed Patch

This morning I went for a walk down our country road. The road ditches were recently mowed, leaving piles of dead grass and weeds along the edge. I noticed a patch of weeds closer to the field, which the mower could not reach. Underneath the dry grass and weeds, pretty wild flowers were blooming. The small wild flowers were a bright colorful spot in the weed patch, like a ray of sunshine on a rainy morning.

I stopped to snap a picture of these tiny flowers. Though my husband calls them weeds, which they are to a farmer, to me there were a symbol of overcoming strife. Some days we feel like a flower in the weed patch, but that doesn't mean we should become hopeless. Our strength and hope are found in Christ. He is the one who helps us bloom in the weed patches.

One of my favorite passages of scripture is *Isaiah 40*, where he speaks of this hope. His words which brought comfort to the people of Jerusalem, are still words of strength for us today. He prophesies of John the Baptist and the coming of the Messiah, who is our hope. *(Isaiah 40:3-5)*.

Our problems here on earth will come and go. There will be days when we resemble a wild flower in a weed patch, as we do our best to blossom. Other days we will wither and fade under the struggles of life, but God's Word is eternal. It is the same yesterday, today and tomorrow.

Isaiah 40 ends with the familiar passage found in *verses 30-31*, but I want you to focus on the verses which lead up to this passage. Yes, the Lord will renew our strength, but we need to understand God's greatness to grasp onto His strength and power. He is all powerful. All knowing. The everlasting Creator. He never grows weary and is the One who cares for you, even when you feel buried beneath the weed patches of life.

"To whom will you compare me? Who is my equal?" asks the Holy One.
Look up into the heavens. Who created all the stars?
He brings them out like an army, one after another, calling each by its name.
Because of his great power and incomparable strength, not a single one is missing.
O Jacob, how can you say the Lord does not see your troubles?
O Israel, how can you say God ignores your rights?
Have you never heard? Have you never understood?
The Lord is the everlasting God, the Creator of all the earth.
He never grows weak or weary.
No one can measure the depths of his understanding.
(Isaiah 40:25-28)

It is difficult to comprehend God with our earthly minds. If you limit your capabilities to earthly knowledge, you will become "*people [who] are like the grass. Their beauty fades as quickly as the flowers in a field." (Isaiah 40:6b).* But when you open your mind and soul to God's omnipotent power, you will find strength and hope. You will not only *"soar high on wings like eagles." (Isaiah 40:31)*. You will bloom in the weed patch of life!

What Do You Believe?

Make allowance for each other's faults, and forgive anyone who offends you. Remember, the Lord forgave you, so you must forgive others. (Colossians 3:13)

Do you ever feel life would be easier if this verse said: "Make allowance for your own faults, and forgive yourself when you offend others. Remember, the Lord forgave them, so you must forgive yourself?"

The truth is, you and I cannot forgive ourselves, only God can forgive us. That is where grace comes in. Jesus forgives us, and because of His grace, we no longer need to carry our burdens.

So it's not a matter of forgiving yourself, the question becomes: What do you believe? If you truly believe that Christ paid the price for your sins on the cross, you have to look past your sins and accept His grace.

None of us live a perfect life. No matter how hard we try, we are going to stumble and fall. Our words can sometimes cut like a knife and hurt the ones we love. On occasion, our actions fall short of the Christian values we know and love. Our past failures, before we believed in Christ, may haunt us. All of these actions make us feel undeserving.

So where do we go from here? According to the writer of *Hebrews 10:17*, once you confess your sins, the slate is wiped clean. Therefore, "forgive yourself"—difficult as it may seem, that is what God commands of us. We are the ones who carry around our guilt, rather than trusting in the blood of Jesus.

It doesn't matter if you are young in your faith, or a mature Christian, you need to walk by faith. Every plateau in your walk with Christ is a step to trust Him more. The more you believe your sins are forgiven, the greater your faith. The stronger your faith, the more victories you will have over Satan. The evil one constantly reminds us of our past failures, but we are given a choice. We can either believe Christ forgives us and wipes the slate clean, or we can choose to believe the evil one and carry around our guilt. *(1 John 2:12-14).*

If we love God, we will accept His Word, because it continually challenges us to overcome evil.

> *"Loving God means keeping his commandments, and his commandments are not burdensome. For every child of God defeats this evil world, and we achieve this victory through our faith. And who can win this battle against the world? Only those who believe that Jesus is the Son of God." (1 John 5:3-5)*

> *But the Lord is faithful; he will strengthen you and guard you from the evil one. (2 Thessalonians 3:3)*

As challenging as it seems, "forgiving oneself" comes down to accepting the grace of Jesus. If you truly believe in the forgiveness of your sins and confess those sins, you are free of guilt. Believe and move forward as a disciple of Christ, because by the grace of God you are free.

> *Then he says, "I will never again remember their sins and lawless deeds." And when sins have been forgiven, there is no need to offer any more sacrifices.*
> *(Hebrews 10:17-18)*

He's My Dad

Fall harvest is underway which makes for busy days. I babysit my granddaughter Reagan two days a week and she goes with the flow in life. She has actually become a great help to me in the kitchen. I cook and hand her sandwiches, chips, cookies, etc. and she packs the lunch boxes. She loves to help and this is a great way to have fun with Grandma.

As we were leaving for the field, she picked up the red lunch box and said, "It's a little heavy, but I'll carry Daddy's lunch, because he's my dad."

What a priceless statement! She melts my heart with her love and kindness for Daddy. We all need to have a "Reagan attitude" in life. I cook and deliver a lot of meals when farming season is in full swing, but I can't always say that I deliver with a "Reagan attitude of kindness." In her case, or the case of a child, kindness comes naturally for those they love. As adults, we tend to lose our kindness when life's struggles and busy schedules cloud our minds and our hearts.

Kindness is mentioned a great deal in the Bible. Often the verses refer to God's kindness such as, *"The Lord is righteous in everything he does; he is filled with kindness." (Psalm 145:17).* On the other hand, Solomon gives us wisdom surrounding kindness in the Proverbs. This wisdom carries forward into the New Testament with kindness being one of the Fruits of the Spirit.

> *But the Holy Spirit produces this kind of fruit in our lives: love, joy, peace, patience, kindness, goodness, faithfulness, gentleness, and self-control. There is no law against these things! (Galatians 5:22-23)*

Kindness is one of the Fruits of the Spirit because it is the nature of Jesus. It was a result of His kindness that we have the opportunity for salvation. *(Titus 3:4-7)*. These fruits of the spirit transform our lives. We can't achieve them on our own, but when we submit our lives to Christ, they become natural. Natural because they are the essence of who Christ is in us. Memorizing the Fruits of the Spirit is not what changes your life. When you allow the Holy Spirit to lead your life, the Fruits of the Spirit become a way of life which you desire. They make a difference in how you live and how you treat others. As you walk this Christian path, you need to submit yourself to God emotionally, physically, socially, and spiritually. Just as Paul writes to the churches of Galatia:

> *Those who belong to Christ Jesus have nailed the passions and desires of their sinful nature to his cross and crucified them there. Since we are living by the Spirit, let us follow the Spirit's leading in every part of our lives. Let us not become conceited, or provoke one another, or be jealous of one another. (Galatians 5:24-26)*

Likewise, let us have a "Reagan attitude" and treat others with the kindness Christ once showed us through the gift of salvation.

Suggested Scripture

- *Proverbs 3:3*
- *Proverbs 11:17*
- *Proverbs 31:26*

Reagan at age 4 carrying Daddy's lunch.

Eyes of a Child

It is often said, "Beauty is in the eye of the beholder," and today was no exception. My granddaughters were picking a bouquet for their mom from the few remaining snapdragon blossoms. I felt as if their bouquet was more stems than flowers, but to them the flowers were beautiful. I mentioned that it was time to cut the marigolds off, but they highly disagreed. I saw a dull brown dying patch of marigolds. They saw beautiful orange and yellow blossoms shining though the darkness.

There are times when we should look at the world through the eyes of a child. They see beauty around themselves and the good in life. As adults, many of us look at the darker side. As we grow older, the simplest of tasks become more difficult and maybe that begins to taint our outlook on life. The struggles we face as adults tend to weigh us down as well. Rather than seeing the beauty in each day, we focus on the work involved, or the negativity surrounding us.

Many women put a great deal of emphasis on their physical beauty. So, the aging process often leaves us feeling less attractive than in our younger days. Peter tells us that our outward beauty should not be a priority in life. Our true beauty comes from within our souls. Since that beauty is from the Holy Spirit, we should never allow it to fade over time. We need to be diligent about caring for our souls in order for our inner beauty to shine.

> *Don't be concerned about the outward beauty of fancy hairstyles, expensive jewelry, or beautiful clothes. You should clothe yourselves instead with the beauty that comes from within, the unfading beauty of a gentle and quiet spirit, which is so precious to God. (1 Peter 3:3-4)*

Is this not the same beauty I mentioned in the previous devotional, *He's My Dad*? *"The unfading beauty of a gentle and quiet spirit,"* is found by heeding the advice given in the Fruits of the Spirit. As a body of believers, our best witness is our attitude in life. If we are quick to argue, or have a bleak outlook on life, we are a poor witness for Christ.

Our lives should reflect the joy of the Lord through our gentle and quiet spirit. The more Christ-like we are, the better witnesses we become. It is often said, "Our actions speak louder than our words." To be a great disciple of Christ, we need to allow the Holy Spirit to fill our hearts with *"love, joy, peace, patience, kindness, goodness, faithfulness, gentleness, and self-control." (Galatians 5:22).*

This devotional book is about the promises of God, and one of His greatest promises is that He will always be with us. *(Matthew 28:20).* God is with you, so look at life through the eyes of a child and see the beauty which surrounds you. Allow yourself to look past the stems to find the snapdragon blossoms and past the dull brown dying marigolds for a glimpse of yellow and orange beauty each day.

Heed My Own Advice

I posted the following quote on Facebook this morning, and then I left home to run multiple errands. While driving from place to place I thought, "I need to heed my own advice and see where God leads me in the Bible today."

> *"For today...allow yourself to read the Bible wherever it opens and concentrate on a verse or two to obtain better knowledge. Ask God to reveal the meaning of those little gems you might have previously overlooked."*
> *~Mary Rodman*[i]

Upon my return, I grabbed my Bible and it opened to the book of Ruth. I was excited because there are many great lessons there, and today was no exception. This verse seemed to jump off the page at me. *"May the Lord, the God of Israel, under whose wings you have come to take refuge, reward you fully for what you have done." (Ruth 2:12).* My immediate thought was, "I sure need refuge from my busy life."

Yes, refuge sounds good today, but my long-distance friend, Leah, needs refuge far more than me. Leah suffers from Osteogenesis Imperfecta (OI), which is a bone and tissue disease. Her OI is in an aggressive state right now and it is affecting her heart. Her symptoms include: chest pains, blocked arteries, shoulder pain, leg pain, low blood pressure, low pulse and more.

I try to say hello to Leah daily, offer her some words of encouragement, and remind her that she is in my prayers. Rather than seeking refuge for myself, my thoughts immediately went to her. I sent her a message and discovered they were ready to start her nuclear stress test. Without hesitation, I replied with *Ruth 2:12* to give her hope and remind her that there is shelter under God's wings.

I then began to pray. My prayers became intermittent as I tried to refocus on writing this devotion. I was unable to concentrate and shed a few tears out of concern for Leah. I later learned that she felt as if she was "losing" and they had to give her two nitro pills to get her through the stress test. She was extremely frightened.

This isn't the first-time Leah and I have felt a connection through the Holy Spirit. It seems odd since we have never met in person, but we have an agape love for one another. Agape love is shown by how we live. When we offer support, encouragement, and Christian friendship, we are expressing agape love because it flows from God, through us, to others.

Ruth had this same agape love for Naomi. When they left Moab, Naomi begged Ruth to return to her homeland. Ruth refused and said, *"Don't ask me to leave you and turn back. Wherever you go, I will go; wherever you live, I will live. Your people will be my people, and your God will be my God."*
(Ruth 1:16).

Ruth held true to her words as they returned to Naomi's homeland of Bethlehem. Not only did Ruth beg to go with Naomi, she cared for her. Ruth was brave as she entered an unfamiliar land, and gleaned from the fields of strangers. She showed love and kindness to everyone, especially Naomi. She worked hard to provide food for the two of them, because she had agape love for her mother-in-law.

Agape love is a love so great, so amazing, and so unstoppable that it trickles through us to others. Today I sought refuge from God as I prayed for Leah. Prayer—what a wonderful gift of agape love. One day I hope to meet Leah in person, but until that day comes, I know under whose wings she can seek refuge, because my God is her God.

Leah and I became acquainted through my first devotional book, ***Bloom Where You're Planted.*** We both agree that God orchestrated our long-distance friendship through unusual God centered circumstances. To read more about our friendship, download the devotion, ***Long-Distance Friends*** from ***Live Life in Full Bloom***, at https://maryrodman.com/landers/book-bonuses-for-bloom-in-god-s-promises

Narrow Hole

I had one of those incidents this week where you look back, chuckle and wonder, "How in the world did that happen?"

I was replacing the hard plastic cover on my cell phone. Hard plastic—that was the problem. I was pushing on the cover to separate the cell phone from it, but I couldn't get them apart. After several attempts and with one very hard push, the cover popped off the phone and onto my thumb. My thumb was now wedged in the camera hole on the case. I no longer had a cell phone case stuck on my phone. I had a cell phone case stuck on my thumb!

You are probably looking at your cell phone case wondering how it could be stuck on my thumb. Your thumb possibly fits through the hole, but God gave me short, stubby fingers. To put this into perspective, my wedding ring is a size 9. My thumb was truly stuck and it was aching!

I tried to twist it off, like I was unscrewing a screw. Bad idea. I didn't make any progress and it wouldn't twist back over my knuckle. I tried a side to side jiggle to get over the knuckle, but had no luck. I pulled, but it didn't want to budge. The more I tried, the more my thumb throbbed. I stopped for a moment and thought about my options. I wondered which would be the least embarrassing: An ER visit to have a cell phone case cut from my thumb, or finding Jim (hubby) to cut it off. Can't you hear people ask, "How did this happened as they tried not to laugh?"

My granddaughter was with me and kept asking, "Are you okay Grandma?"

"Well it hurts, but my thumb went in the hole, so it has to come out, right?"

Before seeking help and to avoid total embarrassment, I gave it one last attempt. I gritted my teeth and pulled the case with as much force as I could. It worked! My thumb was throbbing, and my knuckle was sore for a couple of days. However, the skin was intact and I didn't have to seek help.

My thumb being stuck in a narrow hole reminds me of the words Jesus spoke about the way to heaven.

> *"You can enter God's Kingdom only through the narrow gate. The highway to hell is broad, and its gate is wide for the many who choose that way. But the gateway to life is very narrow and the road is difficult, and only a few ever find it." (Matthew 7:13-14)*

There is no physical narrow road you walk to get into heaven. Jesus is referring to the gift of salvation, which is the only way to heaven. He called it a narrow road because there is no other means of salvation except believing in Him. When you have faith that Jesus carried your sins to the cross, eternity in heaven is a free gift offered to you.

Only Jesus can stand in the gap between you and God to sanctify your sins. When He died on the cross, He took your iniquities upon Himself so you might have eternal life. The road is narrow, but the gift of God's Grace is beautiful and free. All you need to do is confess your sins, and accept His gift of grace. Sadly, many will not believe that Christ is The Way to heaven and pass on this wonderful opportunity of eternal life in heaven.

As Christians, we must remain His faithful disciples, and share the narrow road to heaven with others. You never know, maybe one more push with the great force of prayer, will lead someone down the narrow road to Christ.

Suggested Scripture

- *Matthew 19:23-26*
- *John 10:7-9*

Two Become One

There is a unique maple tree in my neighbor's yard. When the leaves are green in the spring and summer, you would not notice anything unusual about the tree. By all appearances, it is your basic maple tree. But when the leaves change color in the fall, the tree's true beauty shows. One half of the tree is a brilliant orange and the other half is red. When I first observed this unusual sight, I studied the tree a little closer. I noticed the base of the tree has two trunks, but there is only one root system. From all appearances it is one tree, so my guess is that a tree graft didn't work quite properly.

The tree is a symbol of a Christian marriage. There is one root system, Jesus. When a marriage is grounded in Christ, it sustains a couple. Christ is the foundation to grow and lean on in times of trouble. This strong root system allows you to celebrate the joys in life together, but it also gives you the strength to withstand trials as a married couple.

A good Christian marriage functions as one tree. It has one root system—Christ, and two tree trunks—the man and woman joined in marriage. Two separate people who function as one couple. They each have their own gifts and talents, and when God joins them together, He makes something beautiful. *"Therefore a man shall leave his father and mother and be joined to his wife, and they shall become one flesh." (Genesis 2:24 NKJV).*

If one trunk of the maple tree was stronger than the other, it would appear to be two separate trees, but it is one tree. Just as it says in *Ecclesiastes 4:9 (NKJV), "Two are better than one, Because they have a good reward for their labor."* Neither spouse should overpower the other, instead they should work together using the gifts and talents God gave them to build a life as one couple, centered around Christ. *"Each man must love his wife as he loves himself, and the wife must respect her husband." (Ephesians 5:33).*

In the midst of this Christian marriage there will still be days of turmoil and disagreements. On those days remember the wisdom found in *Ephesians 4:32. "Instead, be kind to each other, tenderhearted, forgiving one another, just as God through Christ has forgiven you."*

The Bible is full of wisdom for Christian marriages. The important part of the journey is to keep the roots of your marriage grounded in Christ. When your marriage is centered on the Savior, one person should not outshine the other. You should appear as two brilliant servants of the Lord. One of orange and the other red, but together with Christ you are a triple braided cord and one beautiful tree.

> *Two people are better off than one, for they can help each other succeed. If one person falls, the other can reach out and help. But someone who falls alone is in real trouble. Likewise, two people lying close together can keep each other warm. But how can one be warm alone? A person standing alone can be attacked and defeated, but two can stand back-to-back and conquer. Three are even better, for a triple-braided cord is not easily broken. (Ecclesiastes 4:9-12)*

Suggested Scripture

- *Romans 12:10*
- *Song of Solomon 2:16*
- *Galatians 5:13*

Communication

For the last week or so my husband, Jim, and I have not been able to communicate. We are both engaged in the same conversation, but come to different conclusions. The latest one was a discussion about me following him to the field to help for a few minutes.

He said, "I need to fill the fuel trailer first."

What I heard was, "I need to fill the fuel trailer first, so I will call you when I'm ready for you to come."

In his defense, he never said, "I will call you when I'm ready for you to come." And if I had listened to my granddaughter, she asked me why we didn't go help Grandpa. She obviously listened to the conversation better than me.

An hour or so passed when he called and said, "What happened to you guys? You never showed up."

"Sorry, I thought you were going to call me. What is our problem? It happened again. Why can't we communicate lately?"

Oops—this one was my fault.

Sometimes listening can be difficult. There are too many distractions around us, or too many thoughts rushing through our minds. It doesn't matter if we are listening to our spouse, our children, or God. We need to learn to slow our minds and focus on the conversation we are engaged in.

As a Christian writer and speaker, I am occasionally put up on a pedestal, as if I am sinless and have extra Biblical knowledgeable. Please don't put me up there. I need to confess that my prayer life is the pits right now. I am communicating with God much like I communicated with my husband. I'm only half listening and doing what I feel is right. I have been guilty of saying, *"The Lord has heard my plea; the Lord will answer my prayer." (Psalm 6:9)*, but not truly listening for the Lord's response. I make my own decisions and plow forward as if He granted me permission. How wrong of me!

Many of my devotions are a result of my own humanness. I have a theme as I begin to write, but God changes my thoughts, convicts me, and spins it in a new direction. Today was no different. He pulled me aside and said, "Yes I have heard your plea, but have you listened to my answer?" What a wakeup call from the Lord! I need to go spend some time with the Lord in prayer today.

There are no words left for me to write, except those written by Paul in *2 Corinthians 12:9 (NIV), "But he said to me, 'My grace is sufficient for you, for my power is made perfect in weakness.' Therefore I will boast all the more gladly about my weaknesses, so that Christ's power may rest on me."*

Mindset

Our mind is a garden, our thoughts are the seed, you can grow flowers or you can grow weeds. ~ Unknown

Your mind What controls your mind? I often joke that Jim's mind is full of useless knowledge, simply because he knows countless movie lines, song lyrics and quotes. His useless knowledge lifts my soul, and I can't imagine life without his appropriate sayings in daily life or difficult situations. In spite of any useless knowledge you may or may not possess, your mind is truly a garden.

Your seed The knowledge you input each morning, has a direct effect on your thoughts as your day progresses. So rather than focusing on the latest hype on social media each morning, spend time in God's Word. Meditate on a verse or two which you can apply to your life, your family, or your current circumstances. A good place to start is to read a *Psalm* or *Proverb* each day. You will find words of wisdom such as, *"From a wise mind comes wise speech; the words of the wise are persuasive." (Proverbs 16:23).*

Your flowers Where do you bloom? Our life situations change over the years and we bloom in different situations as we grow older. But regardless of your age, your location, or your circumstances in life, you have a ministry. God gave you gifts and talents along with a deep passion in your soul. This passion or sweet spot, is where you will bloom and grow. Ministry doesn't have to be big and famous, like well-known pastors. Not everyone is called to be a leader in their church either. Ministry can be as simple (or maybe not so simple on those difficult days) as raising your children to love God. Follow the passion God gave you, but remember to plant your roots deep in God's Word.

Your weeds A weed is anything that doesn't come from God, so don't forget to pray. Be bold in your prayers and ask God to thin your weed patch. Satan loves to disrupt your root system when you are doing ministry, so be prepared to withstand his threats. Pray for wisdom, pray for discernment, pray for others, and especially pray for yourself. Don't allow your weeds to choke out the flowers in your life. Stay strong and hold onto your faith.

Ministry can be challenging, even for me as the author of devotions. I have to battle distractions when I'm working, and get frustrated with interruptions. I often forget to pray for wisdom, but God reaches down and helps me out anyway. It is a constant battle to pull up the weeds of negativity, and to push forward with the ministry God has given me. Sometimes I struggle to find just the right scripture, to inspire my readers, but in the end, I remember, *"All scripture is inspired by God and is useful to teach us what is true and to make us realize what is wrong in our lives. It corrects us when we are wrong and teaches us to do what is right. God uses it to prepare and equip his people to do every good work." (2 Timothy 3:16-17).*

I leave you with these three pieces of advice: Fill your mind with seeds from God's Word. Pray and ask God to pull the weeds from your life. Grow and become a flower: especially one cultivated for its beauty.

God or Coincidence

I shared with my publisher, Diane, how our new roof was leading to a new ceiling in our great room. After I described the situation she said, "You are one of the most resilient women I know." I was shocked to hear her say those words, because I definitely didn't feel resilient at the time.

We needed a new roof, and were prepared to handle that expense. But when the roof led to the removal of eleven skylights in our great room, we were a little concerned. We were aware of some condensation problems, but not to the extent of the damage which was uncovered. Not only were the skylights causing problems, the ceiling had serious moisture problems as well. Skylights, drywall, paint, lighting, ceiling fans. Jim and I were seeing $$ as the project continued to spiral out of control!

CONTROL—How can I be resilient when the project is out of control. Out of whose control though? Nothing is too big for God, and we daily prayed about our situation. Yes, Jim and I had a lot of decisions to make, a lot of work to do, and a short time to make everything happen. Yet in the midst of the chaos, God was still in power. Once I grasped that concept, I learned to roll with the punches one day at a time, and yes, I became more resilient.

The Christmas decorations had gone up and I took them back down the same week to prepare for the unexpected remodeling of the living room.

The roofer knew a drywall man and gave him a call. The drywall man had two big jobs pushed back and could easily work us into his schedule when we needed him. God or coincidence?

Jim called an electrician, and he was available the day before the drywall was to be hung. While the carpenters took lunch, he jumped on the scaffold to install the necessary wires and boxes for the new lighting. God or coincidence?

We walked into a lighting store and we both fell in love with the same ceiling fan within minutes. Matching fans were ordered and we were quickly out the door. God or coincidence?

Our sons, Matt and Ryan, were both free this weekend to hang tarps and plastic to block the dust from other rooms, prior to the destruction which began on Monday morning. God or coincidence?

Every step of the way, everything continues to fall into place with God's prefect timing. I didn't need to control the project, because God put the pieces together one step at a time. Releasing control also freed me from the undo stress which I love to put upon myself. Life is always going to have moments of chaos, tragedies, and pain. But life is also filled with joys, triumphs and unnoticed blessings.

Job experienced the agony of losing his family, his possessions, and even his health, but he never lost sight of God, the Giver of all hope. Throughout his discussions with his so-called friends, Job remains strong in his faith of God Almighty. From Job to you and me, God is in control of our lives—from the big projects to the small blessings. He always has us in His powerful arms to comfort us, care for us, and control our destiny.

"But he knows where I am going.
And when he tests me, I will come out as pure as gold.
For I have stayed on God's paths;
I have followed his ways and not turned aside.
I have not departed from his commands,
but have treasured his words more than daily food.
But once he has made his decision, who can change his mind?
Whatever he wants to do, he does.
So he will do to me whatever he has planned.
He controls my destiny."
(Job 23:10-14)

The Missing Light

When we moved into our home thirteen years ago, we discovered a switch which didn't turn any lights or outlets on and off. We finally quit searching, and just ignored it.

The day our living room ceiling was removed during the remodeling project, the carpenter discovered a can light which had never been cut out of the drywall. I promptly handed him a bulb, and once inserted, I flipped the switch. Voila! The mysterious switch does turn on a light, we just didn't have access to it.

The missing light is actually above our front door. I always thought it was odd that there was no light for the entrance, but hey, who am I to question the original builder.

God is our Builder, and He calls us to shine a light on the doorway to heaven. It is our responsibility to introduce others to the gospel. As Christians, if we keep silent or don't reflect Christianity in our lives, how will others know about Jesus?

> *Then Jesus asked them, "Would anyone light a lamp and then put it under a basket or under a bed? Of course not! A lamp is placed on a stand, where its light will shine. For everything that is hidden will eventually be brought into the open, and every secret will be brought to light. Anyone with ears to hear should listen and understand."*
> *(Mark 4:21-23)*

Just like my hidden light fixture created a dark entryway, not showing or expressing your love for Jesus leaves others in the dark. We need to reflect the image of Christ in all we do. Through your day to day actions, through your words, or during those stressful moments—Are you setting a Christian example? At home with your family, in a restaurant, or while driving—Are you setting a Christin example?

We often love the Lord in our private moments, but forget to let our light shine throughout our daily routines. What is keeping you from shining your light? Busyness? Embarrassment? Hardened heart? Fear? Complacency? There are so many reasons why we don't shine our light, but God is very clear about the reason we should brightly shine our light. He wants us to be real and true and not follow the hypocrisy of the Pharisees.

> *"Beware of the yeast of the Pharisees—their hypocrisy. The time is coming when everything that is covered up will be revealed, and all that is secret will be made known to all. Whatever you have said in the dark will be heard in the light, and what you have whispered behind closed doors will be shouted from the housetops for all to hear!" (Luke 12:1b-3)*

The light we shine today, may lead a loved one, an acquaintance, or even a stranger, one step closer to the true Light of the world. Don't hide your light under a basket or even under the drywall. Shine it brightly for a lost world to see!

Favorite Barista

Over time, I have come to know Terri, my favorite barista at the coffee shop. We always enjoy a quick chat while she preps my favorite latte. Even though Terri is ready to stir with a spoon in her hand, nearly every latte bubbles up and overflows the cup. Seldom is she able to make one without having problems. When it overflows, she quickly cleans the cup, apologizes, and passes it my way. Just like my latte cup overflows, Jesus overflows with compassion for His people.

One example of His compassion was near the village of Nain. As Jesus and His disciples traveled toward the village, a large crowd of people began to follow them. When they approached the village gate, they encountered a large funeral procession. This lady had lost her husband and now her only son had died. After the burial of her son, the crowd of mourners would return to their homes, and she would be alone. Sad and alone, possibly bitter, and shedding tears as she worried about the future. Unless a relative was willing to care for her, she would most likely be forced to beg for food, which gave her little hope for the future.

> *When the Lord saw her, his heart overflowed with compassion. "Don't cry!" he said. Then he walked over to the coffin and touched it, and the bearers stopped. "Young man," he said, "I tell you, get up." Then the dead boy sat up and began to talk! And Jesus gave him back to his mother. (Luke 7:13-15)*

What an outward display of compassion for this widow! It wasn't just about the miracle, Jesus spoke words of comfort to her first. In front of a large crowd of mourners and onlookers, Jesus reached out to the lonely widow who was filled with emotions. Her life looked so bleak because of the loss of her family, and Jesus let her know that she was important to Him.

Jesus has the same great compassion for you and I. He is our source of hope when we face tragedies in life, and He is our source of hope when we face small daily struggles. *"His compassions fail not." (Lamentations 3:22 KJV).* Christ will never leave you, and He will never forsake you.

Jesus is a compassionate Savior. He has the ability to bring hope into a lost world. He is concerned about you. The widow. The single mother. The young wife. The lost soul. Christ sees you, the person He created. You are His beloved child and He is wildly passionate about you!

Christ loves you so much that He died on the cross for your sins. Yes, *"his compassions fail not"* and His love for you is unending. As you read the following scripture, sit silently before Jesus and thank Him for who He is, and the sacrifice He compassionately made that you may one day spend eternity in heaven.

> *Though he was God, he did not think of equality with God as something to cling to. Instead, he gave up his divine privileges; he took the humble position of a slave and was born as a human being. When he appeared in human form, he humbled himself in obedience to God and died a criminal's death on a cross. Therefore, God elevated him to the place of highest honor and gave him the name above all other names, that at the name of Jesus every knee should bow, in heaven and on earth and under the earth, and every tongue declare that Jesus Christ is Lord, to the glory of God the Father. (Philippians 2:6-11)*

Ultra-Religious

We recently had the opportunity to be in the audience during a Q&A session with a well-known entertainer. We were enjoying the evening as he shared some of his "behind the scenes" antics and stories from his life. Occasionally he said some classic movie lines, or added a joke to make the evening enjoyable. It was the holiday season and someone asked, "What do you enjoy most about Christmas?"

He grumbled about Christmas in general, and stated that the holiday was way overrated. Then to our shock he said, "Maybe if you are ultra-religious the holiday has more meaning, but to me it is just a hassle." Unfortunately, he received some applause from the audience which saddened my heart.

The more I reflect on his statement, the more it bothers me. I found it very disconcerting that others feel Christmas is a hassle. The holidays have become so commercialized. Gift giving is over emphasized, to the point that we no longer celebrate the true meaning of Christmas. If people feel they have to be ultra-religious to enjoy Christmas, then we as Christians have missed the mark. We are not being the witnesses Christ called us to be. Christmas is about the birth of our Savior. A Savior who changed everything.

> *"This is real love—not that we loved God, but that he loved us and sent his Son as a sacrifice to take away our sins. Dear friends, since God loved us that much, we surely ought to love each other." (1 John 4:10-11)*

> *"Dear children, let's not merely say that we love each other; let us show the truth by our actions. Our actions*

will show that we belong to the truth, so we will be confident when we stand before God." (1 John 3:18-19)

We are called to be confident in our faith. Confident enough to witness about the birth of Christ during the Christmas season! We need to shine a light so bright that others will want to know about our hope which is found in Christ. There is no greater time to be a witness for Jesus than at Christmas.

Often people long to understand the true meaning of Christmas. You have the opportunity to invite them to special Christmas services where they will hear the gospel. You can invite them into your home as you share Christmas traditions, or read the Christmas story to young ones.

We know the truth about the ultimate Christmas gift, the Christ child. Be confident enough in your faith to admit you are ultra-religious and share the true meaning of Christmas with others.

Bible Study Group

I recently joined a Bible study group near my home. A few years ago, these ladies had me as their guest for brunch because they were reading *Bloom Where You're Planted* as a study. They were so sweet and kind, so when they decided to read *Live Life in Full Bloom*, I asked if I could join them. I thought it might be awkward attending as the author of the devotional book they were studying, but they have welcomed me with open arms. A couple of weeks after joining, I arrived about ten minutes late. One lady chuckled and said, "You are one of us now. No one comes on time."

I truly felt like one of the group in just a few weeks. Sometimes we are way off subject, talking about topics which don't seem to relate to the devotionals we read. Other weeks, we are on target as various ladies share how the words impacted their life. In spite of the odd conversations which occasionally come up (like the day we discussed septic tanks), we learn from God's Word together. From chuckles to concerns. From humor to tears. From sick dogs to the passing of loved ones. You will always find support among these ladies. These wonderful sisters in Christ gather from several different churches, and do life together.

As Christians isn't that exactly what God calls us to? I believe Jesus and the disciples enjoyed life together. There had to be some laughter, some tears, some struggles and some joys as they learned from one another. In the gospel of *Luke*, you can read the story of another group of men who did life together.

> *When Jesus returned to Capernaum several days later, the news spread quickly that he was back home. Soon the house where he was staying was so packed with visitors that there was no more room, even outside the door. While he was preaching God's word to them, four men arrived*

carrying a paralyzed man on a mat. They couldn't bring him to Jesus because of the crowd, so they dug a hole through the roof above his head. Then they lowered the man on his mat, right down in front of Jesus. Seeing their faith, Jesus said to the paralyzed man, "My child, your sins are forgiven." (Mark 2:1-5)

The news of Jesus had spread throughout the region, and people were desperate to bring the sick and lame to Him for healing. When there was no way through the crowd to Jesus, they didn't give up and head for home. Instead, they forged ahead. Regardless of the difficulties, they were determined to bring him to Jesus for healing. This short story is packed full of lessons on friendship and helping one another.

Friendship Always be true to your friends. This man obviously had the faith to be healed, but not the means to get to Jesus. His friends helped him, no matter the cost.

Initiative It was creative thinking to lower him through the roof in front of Jesus. God calls us to think outside of the normal parameters. We learn when we are creative.

Faith All of them had faith in Jesus! The scripture doesn't say his faith, it says ***their faith,*** and therefore a miracle happened. When we have faith, and pray as a group, God hears our prayers.

Like these men in Capernaum, we gather each week as friends to study God's Word. The conversations are always creative, whether on target for the lesson or not. Each week our faith resounds as we share our concerns, our joys, our heartaches, our blessings and end in prayer. I truly love this group of ladies who have welcomed me to their Bible study.

I challenge you to do life with a group of friends and study God's Word together. The rewards will be healing for your soul.

Blooming, Budding, Dying

There were huge flowers at our beautiful resort in Costa Rica. I am always drawn to flowers, but this time I saw more than the flowers themselves. I noticed the different stages of the blooms on the bush. There were: buds, blooms and dying flowers, which are each symbols of our walk with Christ.

The budding flower is a stage in our lives when we are searching and longing to be closer to Christ. We sense His presence in an ever so distant manner, and we long to know Him as our true Savior. God desires a personal relationship with us, His children, and purposefully draws us near to Him. *"The Lord looks down from heaven on all mankind to see if there are any who understand, any who seek God." (Psalm 14:2 NIV).*

The dying flower is that horrible stage in your life when God feels distant. You once knew Him and walked with Him daily, but for whatever reason, you no longer sense His daily presence. You may have walked away from the Lord, or sometimes God allows you to walk through the valleys of life, so He can strengthen you. No matter the reason, these days can be difficult, but there are always blessings when you reach the other side of your journey.

On those darkest of days, you need to remember that dying doesn't mean spiritual death. When a bloom dies, it is creating seeds so a new life can begin. Likewise, when you walk through a difficult valley, Christ offers you a new life with Him. *"This means that anyone who belongs to Christ has become a new person. The old life is gone; a new life has begun!"*
(2 Corinthians 5:17).

The beautiful bloom represents your new life with Christ. It doesn't matter if you are a bud searching for Christ, or a dead bloom trying to find your way back. Once you blossom with Jesus, your life will never be the same. You will find joy to shine bright on the darkest days. You will blossom with gladness at the mention of His name. Your blessings will be endless because your life will have purpose, direction, and meaning. So, shout with joy to the Lord today.

Shout with joy to the Lord, all the earth!
Worship the Lord with gladness.
Come before him, singing with joy.
Acknowledge that the Lord is God!
He made us, and we are his.
We are his people, the sheep of his pasture.
Enter his gates with thanksgiving;
go into his courts with praise.
Give thanks to him and praise his name.
For the Lord is good.
His unfailing love continues forever,
and his faithfulness continues to each generation.
(Psalm 100:1-5)

Points to Ponder

- What is your current stage on your journey with Christ?
- Do you feel God calling you into a personal relationship with Him?
- If you feel as if you are walking in the valley, what steps are you taking to draw closer to Jesus?
- How can you spread your joy today?

Unconditional Love

My youngest granddaughter is about two years old. From the day she learned to speak, she has talked nonstop. I don't always understand her words, but there is one phrase which I recognize very clearly, "Hi Grandma!" as she runs toward me with her arms open wide. She melts my heart as she gives me a big hug and lays her head on my shoulder. Kennedy's innocent heart expresses her unconditional love so easily.

Jesus too expresses His unconditional love for us, His children. The scriptures speak of His unfailing love and how nothing can separate us from the love of Christ Jesus. *(Psalms* and *Romans 8:38-39).* His eternal love is an example for us to follow. Love is so important that when the Pharisees questioned Jesus about the greatest commandment, He responded, *"Love the Lord your God."* and *"Love your neighbor as yourself." (Matthew 22:34-39).*

Unconditional love is easy for a child, but adults often find it difficult to love unconditionally. We need to look past their faults, our personal differences, and the unlovable qualities in a person and envision them as a child of God. God's desire is for all of His children to know about the saving grace of Jesus.

Kennedy is a perfect example of love. She wraps her tiny arms around you and holds on tight. Physical touch is often what a person needs, and by all means, love on them! But there is also a different type of love. A love which cares about the person's soul and their eternity.

> *And you must show mercy to those whose faith is wavering. Rescue others by snatching them from the flames of judgment. Show mercy to still others, but do so with great caution, hating the sins that contaminate their lives. (Jude 1:22-23 NIV)*

Those who seem unlovable are often our greatest enemies. No matter how evil they may seem by our worldly standards, they are loved by Jesus. It is often said, "Hate the sin, but love the sinner." The best way to love the sinner, is to share the gospel. Witnessing to the lost is the greatest expression of love one can show. When we share the gospel with the lost, we are truly expressing the love of Christ and fulfilling God's commandment to *"Love your neighbor as yourself."*

Kennedy now age 3 and still melting my heart.

Broken Seashells

While walking the New Smyrna Beach in Florida, I was searching for seashells to give to our grandchildren. I was only able to find a handful of shells which were in good shape, as most of them were broken or chipped. I came upon one particular shell which was intact around the outside, but totally shattered in the middle.

Our lives often reflect the shattered shell. We are holding it together on the outside with our physical appearance looking great. But our soul is telling a completely different story in the middle. What inner turmoil are you hiding from the outside world? What pain and anguish are you hiding from Jesus? Physical pain. Emotional stress. Abuse. Worries and concerns. Loneliness. Depression.

Christ already knows everything about you. He knows all about your shattered life, so don't walk through life alone and miserable. Walk through life with Jesus where you can find hope.

We live in a society which is more concerned with our outward appearance, than our inward brokenness. It doesn't matter what caused your internal pain, you need to be honest with yourself and with God. Allow Him to heal your broken soul.

We are all broken people, and being a Christian doesn't mean that you and I don't suffer. When you feel like your spirit is in the middle of a free-for-all, Christ offers hope. A simple change in your attitude can make a difference. When you stop focusing on your problems, and start focusing on your Healer, you will find comfort for your brokenness.

Dear friend, listen well to my words;
tune your ears to my voice.
Keep my message in plain view at all times.
Concentrate! Learn it by heart!

Those who discover these words live, really live;
body and soul, they're bursting with health.
(Proverbs 4:20-22 MSG)

During his suffering Job said, *"Is not all human life a struggle?" (Job 7:1).* Yet he knew his healing would ultimately come from God Almighty. Like Job, do you believe that God can heal your shattered soul? Dig into His Word for hope and healing. With every Bible verse you read, every step of faith taken, and every prayer you say, God will heal your shattered soul. As healing begins, I pray you will join Job in praying these wonderful words to God.

"I know that you can do anything,
and no one can stop you."
(Job 42:2)

Milestones

I love to reflect on the milestones in my life. It doesn't matter how big or small, an accomplishment is an accomplishment. For example, I had a very successful career with the same company for over twenty years. Big milestone. Writing this devotion today means that *Bloom in God's Promises* is one fourth written. Small milestone. I am grateful for both endeavors.

Upon reflection, I realize it was by God's grace that I was hired by the company in the first place. When Paul interviewed me, I was a struggling single mother with few qualifications for the position. Not only did he take a risk and hire me, he and others patiently mentored me. As a result, my responsibilities increased and my career blossomed.

I'm not an English major, a poet, or a Bible scholar, so writing devotional books is definitely a gift from God. Truth be known, in my previous career I was simply a computer programmer who loved Jesus. While working there, God was preparing me for His greater plan. He continually nudged me to write devotions, and I tucked them away sharing them with only a few people.

God has given me the ability to see Him in my day-to-day routine life, and turn those moments into devotions. It has become my passion. I am blessed to be on this adventure with Him.

As a single mother, I experienced days with almost nothing. Difficult yes, but I am forever grateful for the great profession I was given. There were so many who gave of their time with great patience, while I developed the necessary tools for the job.

I now feel as if I have plenty, living a fulfilled life as I write and speak. Christ has truly blessed me with a wonderful retirement career. Whether I am in want or I have plenty, I will always choose to be grateful for my life.

Like the apostle Paul, I am blessed by the milestones in my life, because without Christ I am nothing.

> *For I have learned how to be content with whatever I have. I know how to live on almost nothing or with everything. I have learned the secret of living in every situation, whether it is with a full stomach or empty, with plenty or little. For I can do everything through Christ, who gives me strength.*
>
> *And this same God who takes care of me will supply all your needs from his glorious riches, which have been given to us in Christ Jesus. Now all glory to God our Father forever and ever! Amen.*
> *(Philippians 4:11b-14,19-20)*

I eagerly look forward to more accomplishments in my life. Each step, whether a struggle or an achievement, is a *blessing* from God. Each *blessing* leads me to a *deeper relationship* with Jesus. A *deeper relationship* with Jesus fills my heart with *gratitude*.

Reflect on the milestones in your life. Your heart will be filled with gratitude because Jesus fulfills your every need.

Intense Fellowship

A couple of small issues were building between Jim and I, until I finally had a slight explosion today. When I aired my frustration with him, we had a moment of "intense fellowship." There were no harsh words, and I feel better about both situations. We both agreed to disagree on one issue, and on the other he apologized. Life is now good again at the Rodman household.

I wasn't out to start a fight today, but after much thought, I felt that Jim should know he hurt my feelings. I had no intention of putting the blame on him, but needed to express what was in my heart. The outcome was good—a very sincere apology. I chose not to bury my anger knowing that one day it would probably bubble to the surface over something totally unrelated.

When we agreed to disagree, it was a gesture of love for both of us. In marriage and in life, there will always be disagreements, but when no solution is reached, a truce is the Christian way.

Before moments of "intense fellowship," do you pick your battles wisely? It is often difficult to ignore your own feelings when an argument ensues. The disagreement can be within your family, your workplace and even your church. In his letter to the church of Ephesus, Paul urges the church to lead a life of unity. These strong Christian values should be applied when "intense fellowship" occurs as well.

> *Therefore I, a prisoner for serving the Lord, beg you to lead a life worthy of your calling, for you have been called by God. Always be humble and gentle. Be patient with each other, making allowance for each other's faults because of your love. Make every effort to keep yourselves united in the Spirit, binding yourselves together with*

peace. For there is one body and one Spirit, just as you have been called to one glorious hope for the future. (Ephesians 4:1-4)

As a Christian, we are called to lead a life based on the values established in these verses. Be humble, gentle, patient and understanding. Not just when life is going your way, but when disputes arise as well.

If you are continually having "intense fellowship" with others, maybe you need to evaluate your heart. Are you displaying these values in your life? There is definitely a time and a place to express your hurt, your pain, and your opinion, but choose your battles wisely. Evaluate the true reason for your unhappiness before striking out in anger.

Life is often about disagreements, broken hearts and compromises. Rather than dealing with these situations in anger, choose to start with a humble, gentle, patient and understanding spirit. With prayer, patience, and practice, your moments of "intense fellowship" will become acts of Christian love and understanding.

501C3

Since the first of the year there has been a new joke at our house. I told Jim that I need to file a 501C3 tax form to become a non-profit organization so he can write me off on our taxes. Interpretation—publishing two books last year hasn't been very profitable for me. In all seriousness, profit isn't my main goal in this business, though self-sustaining would be a nice target for 2020.

All joking aside, making that comment has forced me to look at what my true purpose is as a Christian author and speaker. Over the past several years I have gained a small group of avid followers, which actually surprises me. I always wonder what I say that brings them back for more. (If you are one of those people, please send me some feedback and let me know.) One thing I am sure of is that God and I are in this together.

He is with me during those sleepless nights. (It is 1:00 am right now.) He is with me in the triumphs. He is with me when the words just don't seem to flow. And I beg Him to tag along when I have to play the role of sales and marketing. (My least favorite part.) So why do I do what I do?

First and foremost, it is conviction to use my gifts to help fulfill the Great Commission. *(Matthew 28:16-20).* We are all called to be disciples and share the gospel. My calling is to write and share the stories of my life, which I intertwine with the God's Word. Hopefully by reading my devotions, you become more aware of Christ's presence, even on the mundane and crazy days.

Second, *"Well done, my good and faithful servant." (Matthew 25:21)*. One day I will stand before the Lord and I long to hear those words, *"Well done."* I know without a shadow of doubt that this ministry is what God has called me to do. So, I can spend a sleepless night (like tonight) tossing and turning, or I can get out of bed and put the thoughts spinning in my head into my Word document. (If you had a vision of me with a pen and paper, writing each devotion, sorry to burst your bubble. I do scribble a lot of notes on random pieces of paper though.) Not all of my words are written in the middle of the night, but it does happen. I have learned to seize the moment when God sends a message.

Why do I seize the moment—to offer you encouragement. I have always felt that encouragement is the number one goal of my messages. Life happens, and whether my story is sad, comical, or just my humdrum life, relating those moments to scripture is where I find encouragement for my life. In turn I share those glimpses of encouragement, faith, and hope with you. My goal is to help you *Bloom in God's Promises*.

In closing here is one of my favorite verses which I have used many times. *"When we get together, I want to encourage you in your faith, but I also want to be encouraged by yours." (Romans1:12).* So, if you are having a sleepless night too, send me some words of encouragement on Facebook or email! I may be awake and respond.

Junk

My publisher, Diane, offered me an opportunity to become a part of a new project. I am excited about the prospect of being the first author in the *Inspire U* app, but of course no venture comes without a price. I prayed about the opportunity and talked to Jim concerning the cost involved. As I said in the previous devotional, *501C3*, I am trying to be self-sustaining in 2020, and want to stay within my budget.

Jim's response was, "I just sold some junk. You can have the money."

I appreciate his offer for the money, but hope he isn't insinuating anything by giving me "junk" money. His junk is actually old farm equipment and miscellaneous items which he recently sold on a farm auction. So, there is no actual trash involved, just a little rust, dirt and grime.

We all have junk in our lives. Possibly the rust of a shady past, which chips away at our self-worth. We wonder how God could ever use us as a witness with all of our rusty holes. Often dirt rolls from our tongues when anger or frustrations build in our lives. Our minds may also be filled with dirt, as we think non-Christian thoughts about others. Grime—layers and layers of sins. Some sins we confess and others we may never acknowledge.

The story of Joseph can be found in the book of Genesis. Joseph's brothers were filled with junk. They turned on Joseph when he was seventeen years old. Can you imagine the words which rolled from their tongues on that fateful day? Accusations about him being the favorite son. Hatred and a plan to murder him. Instead, they threw him into a well to die and intended to leave him there. Some Egyptian traders came along and they decided to sell him into slavery instead. They didn't want his blood on their conscious, yet they were willing to deceive their father about what happened to Joseph. For years, the brothers lived with guilt because of their actions. Layers and layers of rust, dirt and grime.

Approximately two decades passed before Joseph saw his brothers again. Due to the famine in the country his brothers came to Egypt to purchase food. On their second trip for food, Joseph revealed his identity to them. They are scared and afraid. Their dirty, rusty, grimy past flashed before them as they feared the worst. Would Joseph seek retaliation for what they had said and done to him? Instead of vengeance, Joseph said:

> *"But don't be upset, and don't be angry with yourselves for selling me to this place. It was God who sent me here ahead of you to preserve your lives. This famine that has ravaged the land for two years will last five more years, and there will be neither plowing nor harvesting. God has sent me ahead of you to keep you and your families alive and to preserve many survivors. So it was God who sent me here, not you! And he is the one who made me an adviser to Pharaoh—the manager of his entire palace and the governor of all Egypt." (Genesis 45:5-8)*

Joseph was ridiculed, shunned, and sold by his brothers. He had experienced hatred, anger, and neglect. But he also understood the meaning of God's love, and His wondrous plan. When Joseph was sold to the Egyptians, God had a plan. Joseph chose to look past the rust, dirt, and grime of his brothers and allow himself to be used by God.

Jim's rusty, dirty, grimy junk money may be part of God's plan. I need to look past my own personal junk of being a self-sustaining ministry and focus on God's will for this venture.

Like Joseph's brothers, does all of your rusty, dirty, grimy junk continuously flash through your mind? God wastes nothing in our lives. He will one day turn all of your junk into a glorious plan to better His kingdom. Allow God to turn your rusty, dirty, grimy life into something spectacular!

Create Memories

> The following devotion was written in the midst of the coronavirus pandemic. Though the peak of the pandemic is over, the lesson remains the same.

God created us with amazing senses—sight, hearing, taste, smell and touch. Each of our senses work separately, yet they also work together. For example, a blind person typically has a greater sense of hearing and touch to compensate for the loss of their vision. But even though their other senses are heightened, it will never totally replace their loss of sight.

Our senses can often cause us to experience flashbacks of great memories. While driving last week, I could smell smoke in the air. It wasn't the smell of trash or leaves burning, but the smell of wood. I looked around and saw smoke billowing from the chimney as I passed a house. I instantly had a flashback to my childhood.

The smell in the air was the exact aroma of the wood furnace which heated our home. I took in a deep breath as wonderful memories flooded my mind. I had a vision of my sister and I standing on a warm register vent after being outside in the cold. Possibly we had helped Dad cut the wood which kept us warm. I remembered family nights filled with playing cards, games, and puzzles in the warm cozy living room. I had a moment of nostalgia as one memory after another flooded my mind. All a result of smelling the smoky air.

The coronavirus has changed our lives. Rather than worrying about of the situation, create some great memories with your family. Like the smell of wood burning, one day your senses will remind you of the wonderful days spent together at home.

Instead of watching the news 24/7 and stressing about social distancing, spend your energy creating family fun.

One day you will recall the laughter you shared, but not the news cast. Possibly the wonderful smell of a home cooked meal will bring you back to the day you prepared a meal as a family project. You will have flashbacks of the hugs of loved ones, but not the daily statistics on the news. The sounds of your children playing, laughing, fighting, and sharing will one day seem so distant as they grow up all too quickly.

For those you of who live alone, special projects will one day resonate in your heart long after the fear is gone. Create your own memories by reading, calling loved ones, or cooking yourself a special meal.

Every memory is a blessing, and every blessing is a God moment in your life.

There are childhood memories, memories of a national pandemic, and there are also God memories. The Israelites had wandered in the dessert searching for the Promised Land. When God gave them the Ten Commandments, they heard His voice at the foot of the mountain. Moses urged the Israelites to never forget the wonderful God moments they experienced throughout their journey.

> *"But watch out! Be careful never to forget what you yourself have seen. Do not let these memories escape from your mind as long as you live! And be sure to pass them on to your children and grandchildren. Never forget the day when you stood before the Lord your God at Mount Sinai, where he told me, 'Summon the people before me, and I will personally instruct them. Then they will learn to fear me as long as they live, and they will teach their children to fear me also.'" (Deuteronomy 4:9-10)*

Like the Israelites, you are creating God moments to share. One of the greatest impacts you can have on the unsaved or the next generation is to share your God moments. We can walk the walk of a Christian, but until we learn to talk the talk, how will others ever understand our blind faith in Jesus! Contemplate these questions: How are you persevering on these difficult days? How has your faith impacted your ability to cope? What prayers have you said on behalf of your loved ones?

We all have a faith journey which needs to become part of our testimony. I challenge you to share your testimony on my blog today. It doesn't matter how simple or complex your message is. What is important is to share your message of encouragement with others. Never allow your God moments to stay hidden in your heart. They are memories which are meant to be shared with the world!

Go to www.MaryRodman.com/Blog to read my post ***Have Faith and Pray.*** Please share your faith story in the comments so others will be encouraged by your testimony.

BMV Day

Our county BMV office has a reputation for being rude to their customers. I understand that the state of Ohio requires specific paperwork, but a little assistance from the clerks would be a great help. The first frustration is that no one ever makes just one trip to the office. You will be missing some appropriate paperwork, possibly a social security card, a passport, proof of residence or other paperwork they deem necessary. The second frustration is the long line. It can be so frustrating that we should wave flags that say "BMV day" so our friends and family know we will be in a bad mood and to keep a clear distance.

On my fist trip to the office, I was missing proof of residence. The clerk shoved a paper at me with the requirements, and hollered for the next person in line. I closely read the list of requirements and returned a few days later. My stack of papers included a quarterly investment summary, which was on the list of acceptable documents for proof of residence. My paperwork was denied because the word "statement" was not on the paper. It was obvious that it was a statement by the financial information and dates listed. This is when my anger began.

To make a long story short, rather than holding up the line, I requested my paperwork back from the clerk and I turned to walk away. The clerk rudely yelled from behind the desk, "It's not my fault it is the government."

I angrily replied, "No it is your fault, because you won't accept a valid document."

I quickly stormed out in anger, before I cleared the BMV office like Jesus cleared the temple.

After venting to my husband and my sister, I went to a different BMV office. I was amazed at the friendliness of the clerks. There were no harsh words. No arguments. No frustrations.

I even witnessed a clerk who took the time to explain to a young girl the necessary steps to reestablish her suspended license. What a difference a clerk's attitude made in the experience! I actually left a BMV office with a smile on my face and thanked her for her friendly attitude.

When all is said and done, life is about choices. I chose to allow the situation to make me angry. I'm not happy about my attitude or my words as I stormed out of the office. I definitely did not act like a Christian and turn the other cheek, when I was denied my driver's license renewal. *(Matthew 5:38-40)*. Hopefully in the future I will choose wisely. I can choose which BMV office to do my business and I can choose a better attitude.

There is one lesson we can all learn from frustrating situations such as this. Your attitude trickles into the lives of those around you. If you have a frustrating job or a frustrating situation like the BMV, don't allow your attitude to impact others. Life is about choices, so chose to live your life worthy of the words written in *Philippians 2:4-5. "Don't look out only for your own interests, but take an interest in others, too. You must have the same attitude that Christ Jesus had."*

Mighty Oak

The mighty oak was once a little nut that stood its ground.
~Unknown

This was the fortune inside my cookie one day. I thought it was inspirational so I taped it to my notebook and refer to it from time to time. By now, you have read enough devotions to know that I am a little nutty at times. Not everyone titles their devotionals, "O Man!," "Trash," and "Bird Poop." God gives me the ability to see Him in every aspect of my life. I just call it like I see it, or in this case, write it like I see it.

The good news is that I am not the only nut who follows her calling from God. The Bible is full of nut cases, or at least other people thought they were crazy. The story of David and Goliath for example How many people supported David's decision to fight the giant? Not a single one. Even Saul told him he was crazy when he volunteered to fight Goliath. *(1 Samuel 17:33).* However, David knew the Lord was with him and declared victory over Goliath before the battle began by saying, *"This is the Lord's battle, and he will give you to us!"*
(1 Samuel 17:47).

Did you ever think of Noah as a nut case? God told Noah to build an ark and it had never rained before! No doubt he was ridiculed and thought to be crazy by everyone. Since God only spoke to Noah, was his wife supportive? Did Shem, Ham and Japheth help build the ark without questions? It took years and years to build the ark, in that time frame did Noah ever question God? *Genesis 6:9* says, *"Noah was a righteous man, the only blameless person living on earth at the time, and he walked in close fellowship with God."*

When God called Noah righteous and blameless, He was not saying that Noah was sinless. It means he loved the Lord with all his heart. He walked so closely with God that he made it into the faith Hall of Fame in *Hebrews 11*!

> *It was by faith that Noah built a large boat to save his family from the flood. He obeyed God, who warned him about things that had never happened before. By his faith Noah condemned the rest of the world, and he received the righteousness that comes by faith. (Hebrews 11:7)*

There is no doubt Noah experienced rejection from others when he began to build an ark on dry land. Regardless of their sneers, harsh words, and rejection, Noah chose to follow God's command.

As Christians, we are often looked upon as different or peculiar for our beliefs and actions. There are times when our obedience to God makes others look disobedient. Their natural reaction is to flip the situation around and make us look like the nutty ones. When those situations arise, just remember what Noah overcame. God will always give you the strength to complete the job.

This nut case has stood her ground, sometimes a result of perseverance, but mostly out of love for Jesus. Not everyone loves my books, and not everyone understands why I write devotions on topics like "Bird Poop" or "Toilet." What I do know is this, I am a little nut in a big sea of authors. When I stand my ground, and write the words God gives me, I become a mighty oak in God's eyes, and that is what is most important.

Prayer Police

My granddaughter Reagan has learned to pray before eating her snack at preschool. So now at mealtime, Reagan patiently waits for the prayer to be said. Her sister, Mya, however is not so patient. She is always starving (just ask her) and dives in as quickly as possible.

Reagan has earned the nickname of Prayer Police because she always says, “Mya is eating before we prayed.”

I don’t like to encourage tattling, but I love how at the age of four, Reagan has become an influencer. Generally, Mya will put down her fork, acknowledge her mistake, and wait for the prayer before she continues.

I was not a Christian influencer at the age of four, and there are days as an adult I still miss the mark. As Christians, we sometimes find it easier to go with society, rather than standing up for our beliefs and our values.

Jeremiah understood how the pressures of society could be a bad influence. Following the evil reign of Manasseh, Judah had become very corrupt. The people knew the importance of God’s blessing, but refused to change their ways to receive it. They continued their evil practices, but didn’t understand why God’s wrath was upon them. As God’s prophet, Jeremiah was caught in the middle. He prayed for Judah, but the people of Judah hated him. Jeremiah feared for his life as Judah continued to rebel against God.

Regardless of their hatred toward him, Jeremiah continued to pray. But, *“He [God] had decided to banish Judah from his presence because of the many sins of Manasseh, who had filled Jerusalem with innocent blood. The Lord would not forgive this.” (2 Kings 24:3b-4).*

Jeremiah was afraid of the people of Judah. They had rejected him as a prophet to pursue their evil ways. He felt abandoned by God and was even angry at Him because his prayers could not change God's heart. If God would no longer allow him to intercede for Judah, what was his purpose on earth?

> *This is how the Lord responds: "If you return to me, I will restore you so you can continue to serve me. If you speak good words rather than worthless ones, you will be my spokesman.* ***You must influence them; do not let them influence you!*** *They will fight against you like an attacking army, but I will make you as secure as a fortified wall of bronze. They will not conquer you, for I am with you to protect and rescue you. I, the Lord, have spoken! Yes, I will certainly keep you safe from these wicked men. I will rescue you from their cruel hands."*
> *(Jeremiah 15:19-21 Emphasis added)*

We are often caught in the middle like Jeremiah. Between good and evil. Right and wrong. Godly and ungodly. When we are in these circumstances, God calls us to be an influencer, not a follower. Our reward is His protection on earth and eternity in heaven.

I am proud of my prayer police granddaughter. She isn't praying for Judah, but she is making an impact for Jesus in her small little world. I challenge you to become the prayer police in your small piece of the world too.

Mary Rodman

Just Wait

Prayer is the pause that empowers. ~Unknown

It had been a busy day when I checked my email account for the first time. The first email was a book order from Pam. I had a wow moment, because Pam had just ordered a few weeks before. I glanced at the clock and realized the post office was open for another thirty minutes. I quickly packed the order, grabbed my keys and went to the post office. I mailed the envelope of books to Pam with a smile on my face excited about her additional order.

Upon my return, I logged onto my computer again to do the necessary paperwork to complete the order. That is when I realized it was the same order I had filled for Pam before. (Head slap.) Obviously, I had forgotten to delete her previous email. I never looked at the date on the email, all that ran through my mind was that the post office was about to close.

Since the package was already on its way, I sent Pam an email admitting the error of my ways. I informed her that she would receive her order…again. I told her to give the books to friends, or family members who would enjoy them, or even donate them to a church or library. Pam probably had a good chuckle as she read the email, and hopefully didn't question my sanity.

I often make mistakes like this when I am super busy. I forget to slow myself long enough to focus. But God uses all of our mistakes in life, and in this scenario, I'm sure God has a plan. Pam will know where to share the books, so they impact lives in Utah.

Why do I live in such a whirlwind some days? I have moments of sleeplessness and I make crazy mistakes…like shipping books twice. I am forgetful of conversations (just ask my husband). And yes, sometimes I can't even focus to pray.

While writing this devotion, I was searching for scripture to tie to my story. I did a BibleGateway.com search for crazy lady, but there was no reference found. I asked Jim for suggestions, and though he had some good ideas, none of them seemed to quite fit.

I repeatedly asked God, "What message am I to share with my readers?"

The answer I heard over and over again from God, was "Wait."

"Wait for what God?"

"Just wait."

We often want the answers instantly, but God calls us to wait, and so I waited. Following a few moments of quiet prayer and reflection I began to flip through my Bible. I stopped to read numerous passages which were wonderful, yet unrelated to the story. All I could sense in my spirit was "wait."

"Wait for what God?"

"Be still and just wait."

"But I have used *Psalm 46:10, "Be still and know that I am God,"* so many times Lord.

Again, "Just wait."

I flipped through more scriptures and suddenly God's message became very clear. I was waiting for Him to give me that "Ah ha moment." He was waiting for me! I was the one who was running from scripture to scripture. Idea to idea. Spinning like a crazy woman looking for answers, when all He wanted was for me to spend time with Him.

> *"So the Lord must wait for you to come to him so he can show you his love and compassion. For the Lord is a faithful God. Blessed are those who wait for his help." (Isaiah 30:18)*

There it was! “Just wait.”
If you find yourself frazzled today. “Just wait.”
If you have a sleepless night. “Just wait.”
If your life is spinning out of control. “Just wait.”
Life’s problems are solved when we, “Just wait.”

Missing Dad

The coronavirus lock down is taking a toll on many people. I don't mind being home, but it bothers me that I can't visit Dad at assisted living. I trust the staff to meet his every need and am thankful that he is still pretty self-sufficient. He needs a few reminders now and then, but remains active. You will find him at bingo or a euchre game when possible, and sometimes he is out for a ride in their van.

He often sits near the front door where he can watch people come and go. Yesterday on my way to the store for a few essentials, I made a quick stop at Bluebird Retirement Center. I knew I couldn't actually go in and visit, but I was hoping for a glimpse of him by the door. He was there, so I frantically waved hello as I passed in an envelope containing handmade cards from his great-grandchildren and a short note from me.

Dad heard my voice and started to come toward the door. I quickly told him no and reminded him that I couldn't come in. I let him know we were all doing fine and waved goodbye. As I turned to walk away, tears filled my eyes. I knew social distancing wasn't going to be easy for any of us, but I didn't realize just how much I would miss Dad.

Isn't it funny how you don't miss something until it is gone? Dad isn't gone, but yet I long to visit with him. Regular visits were part of my routine. I sit and chatter about things happening on the farm, and he listens. Sometimes I play bingo or euchre with him, or even stay for a meal. I am anxious for the social distancing to be over, so I can spend more precious time with him.

This pandemic has taught me to focus on one important lesson in life. Don't ever let your busy schedule keep you from precious time with loved ones. There will be days, like this period of social distancing, when you long for time together. Time is the one item we can never get back. Once a moment is lost, it is lost forever. One day I will truly look back and realize how many priceless minutes I have missed with friends and family, for one reason or another.

Solomon in all his wisdom wrote beautiful words to describe time. No matter how many times we read them, something new will always touch our hearts. Remember to always use your time wisely, because time is a precious commodity. Don't waste it.

For everything there is a season,
a time for every activity under heaven.
A time to be born and a time to die.
A time to plant and a time to harvest.
A time to kill and a time to heal.
A time to tear down and a time to build up.
A time to cry and a time to laugh.
A time to grieve and a time to dance.
A time to scatter stones and a time to gather stones.
A time to embrace and a time to turn away.
A time to search and a time to quit searching.
A time to keep and a time to throw away.
A time to tear and a time to mend.
A time to be quiet and a time to speak.
A time to love and a time to hate.
A time for war and a time for peace.
(Ecclesiastes 3:1-8)

Mr. Bluebird

Despair comes from not knowing this is not our home.
~Unknown

Spring is in the air, and I love it. The grass is turning green. The daffodils have buds, and will soon have flowers. The birds are singing. The killdeer is scurrying to hide its nest along the drive. I love the first signs of spring, and the beginning of new growth.

Among all of this beauty, I have one pest. A bluebird who has banged on my office window for several days. Occasionally he perches on the edge of the window gazing in, as if he is longing for a home. We tried to help him out and cleaned the sparrow nest out of the bluebird house, but it didn't help.

There are several theories on why birds knock on windows, but the main one is that they are territorial during the mating season. According to the internet, once they find a mate, they will cease. (I haven't seen him this morning, so maybe he has a girlfriend finally.) Regardless, he is a persistent little fellow. No matter how many times he has hit the window, pecked the window, or perched on the window, and even fallen to the ground, he returns all day long.

Persistence is a lesson we can learn from Mr. Bluebird. Regardless of our difficulties in life, we need to steadfastly pray to Jesus, our source of hope.

Your days may be filled with despair. Who is your source of hope? Jesus.

Life may seem miserable or you may feel forsaken. Who is your source of hope? Jesus.

Has your life been one trial after another? Jesus is your source of hope.

Can we even compare our sufferings to that of the apostle Paul? As an early apostle, he suffered opposition, imprisonment, and physical beatings. Yet he was able to continuously encourage others. He wrote the Corinthians, the church of Ephesus, the Galatians, and many others a countless number of letters. He encouraged them to persevere, and consistently reminded them that their hope was found in Jesus. He gave of himself for the benefit of gospel.

Like Mr. Bluebird and Paul, we need to persevere, regardless of the difficulties in life. Remembering that our hope is found in Jesus Christ too.

> *We now have this light shining in our hearts, but we ourselves are like fragile clay jars containing this great treasure. This makes it clear that our great power is from God, not from ourselves. We are pressed on every side by troubles, but we are not crushed. We are perplexed, but not driven to despair. We are hunted down, but never abandoned by God. We get knocked down, but we are not destroyed. (2 Corinthians 4:7-9)*

We have the ability to rely on the Holy Spirit for hope and guidance just like Paul did. Even though our lives are like fragile clay jars, we have the hope of eternity with Christ. Difficulties will come and go, but persistence will see us through. We may feel miserable and in despair, but spring is coming and new growth will arrive. Like Mr. Bluebird, you may get knocked down, but you are not destroyed, because Jesus has overcome, and He is our great source of hope!

> *"That is why we never give up... We fix our gaze on things that cannot be seen. For the things we see now will soon be gone, but the things we cannot see will last forever.*
> *(2 Corinthians 4:16a, 18b)*

Mary Rodman

God's Favor

I was taking my granddaughters to school, and as usual I lost track of time that morning. We rushed out the door in a flurry so they wouldn't be late. Mya and I dropped Reagan off at preschool, and she was next. We always have a little bit of time to kill and often stop at the coffee shop for our usual smoothie and latte.

In my rush to get Reagan to school on time, I didn't go to the bathroom before I left home. I left Mya waiting for our drinks and went to the restroom. I flopped my purse on the corner of the sink and went about my business. I heard water running which didn't make any sense. I looked up and had a moment of panic! My purse had fallen into the sink which had an automatic water faucet. The water was running directly into the side pocket of my purse, which of course contained my cell phone.

I was frantic. I couldn't reach my purse because it was too far away, and I couldn't just get up either. (I think you know what I mean. You can't just stop once you start.) All I could do was wait it out and hope for the best. As soon as I completed my business, I grabbed my purse out of the sink, turned it upside down and poured a pocketful of water down the drain.

Next problem—no paper towels. The restroom had automatic hand driers and I let out a sigh. I dried my cell phone and purse as best I could with my jacket and jeans and exited the restroom. I was too embarrassed to explain to the barista why I looked like I had just showered. She knows me because I am a frequent customer, so how embarrassing would that be! (Later I realized she would have enjoyed a good chuckle and I should have shared my mishap.)

Mya and I grabbed our drinks and off we went to school. I checked my phone again while we were in the drop off line at school. It still worked! I don't know why my cell phone worked after sitting in a purse full of water, but it did.

Maybe I do know why. Sometimes God just gives us a little bit of His favor. It is the only explanation that makes any sense, because a phone sitting in water should definitely have issues, and it doesn't. God probably looked down and thought, "She does her best to spread a little Christian love. I think I will show her some favor today."

At the end of the day, I am thankful for a working cell phone. I am even more grateful that God pours out His kindness and favor upon us. We often take for granted God's faithfulness, yet He continues to be merciful and compassionate to those who seek Him.

Focus on the favor of God today. Say a prayer of thanks and acknowledge the goodness He has bestowed upon you. He will lift your spirits and continue to bless your life. A time of reflection will give you a heart full of gratitude and more love for the Giver of great favor.

God always does what he says,
and is gracious in everything he does.
Generous to a fault,
you lavish your favor on all creatures.
Everything God does is right—
the trademark on all his works is love.
God's there, listening for all who pray,
for all who pray and mean it.
He does what's best for those who fear him—
hears them call out, and saves them.
God sticks by all who love him,
but it's all over for those who don't.
My mouth is filled with God's praise.
Let everything living bless him,
bless his holy name from now to eternity!
(Psalm 145:13b,16-21 MSG Emphasis added)

Deposits

Our grandchildren each have a piggybank at our house. A way to teach them how to save a little money. The oldest two grandkids no longer ask for money. They just go to the money basket and help themselves. I joke about them stealing money, but they know the change basket is for them.

Their favorite part of this venture is when they deposit their money at the bank. They dump their money into the change counting machine, and proudly give their receipts to the teller to make a deposit. Our local bank has a treasure chest full of great prizes which is more incentive for them to save money. They give the bank $10, and the bank gives them a 10-cent trinket. Reagan soon figured out that she could ask Grandma for cash while at the bank and that worked too. She didn't have to empty her piggybank to make a deposit and get a trinket. She is one smart 4-year-old, who has Grandma wrapped around her little finger!

There are more ways to make deposits in life than monetary ones. One can deposit into the lives of family by showing unconditional love. Listening to the woes of a friend will deposit trust into the relationship. Prayer and meditation with the Lord, deposits hope, faith, and strength into your own life.

Jeremiah was surrounded by sin and sorrow. Jerusalem had been destroyed by Babylon, and the people had either been killed or taken captive. In the midst of all his grief he wrote the book of Lamentations. Regardless of the evil around him, Jeremiah saw a ray of hope and renewed his faith in God. Prior to Jerusalem's destruction, he had made deposit, after deposit. Prayer after prayer. He spent time with the Lord day after day. Now all of those deposits were his source of strength on the darkest of days.

The thought of my suffering and homelessness is bitter beyond words.
I will never forget this awful time, as I grieve over my loss.
Yet I still dare to hope when I remember this:
The faithful love of the Lord never ends! His mercies never cease.
Great is his faithfulness; his mercies begin afresh each morning.
I say to myself, "The Lord is my inheritance; therefore, I will hope in him!"
The Lord is good to those who depend on him, to those who search for him.
So it is good to wait quietly for salvation from the Lord.
(Lamentations 3:19-26)

Remember, Reagan didn't have to empty her piggybank to make a deposit, and the same is true with God. You always have a full account. It is not a give and take system where you put one prayer in, and get a 10-cent trinket of hope back. Your deposits can be endless, and your withdrawals are priceless and never-ending.

Our hope will never cease when we put our trust in El Roi, the God who sees us. He sees us in times of sorrow and in times of happiness. He is forever a passionate, caring, and loving God who gives us hope, faith and strength with each withdrawal. *Great is his faithfulness; his mercies begin afresh each morning. (Lamentations 3:23).*

Spring Day

Spring is in the air! What a great feeling, but unfortunately every day is not spring-like weather in Ohio. A few days ago, we had a beautiful spring day—sunshine, warm weather, birds singing, flowers blooming—all the wonderful signs of spring. Our beautiful spring day was followed by thunderstorms and high winds. Now today, we are back to cold, cloudy, windy weather. Regardless of the temperatures, spring is in the air, which means spring jobs need completed.

The best time to roll the lawn is following a heavy spring rain, which we just had. So crazy me, I decided to roll the lawn this morning. I bundled in my hoodie, coat, gloves, and boots, and grabbed my iPod for music. The music was a great idea as it distracted me from the cold temperatures.

The first swipe across the lawn was into the wind and I almost retreated to the house. Once I turned it didn't seem as bad, so I persevered. I went back and forth, and crisscross on the worst sections of the lawn. I endured long enough to roll the lawn one or two times, depending on the area. I felt a sense of accomplishment as I parked in the barn. I had checked one more spring item off of the spring "to-do-list."

Why is it that once you feel the warmth of your home, you suddenly realize exactly how chilled you are? As I unbundled, I began to shiver. I have been in the house for three hours and I'm still trying to get warm. There just isn't enough hot tea to warm this cold body this afternoon.

Fortunately, there are ways to warm my spirit, even though my physical body is cold. So along with that second cup of hot tea, I read my daily devotions. Today's lesson talked about the New Heaven and the New Earth. Oh, how our earthly chilled bodies long to be with God one day. What a warm thought, We will one day spend eternity in heaven with Immanuel, which means "God is with us."

> *Then I saw a new heaven and a new earth, for the old heaven and the old earth had disappeared. And the sea was also gone. And I saw the holy city, the new Jerusalem, coming down from God out of heaven like a bride beautifully dressed for her husband. I heard a loud shout from the throne, saying, "Look, God's home is now among his people! He will live with them, and they will be his people. God himself will be with them."*
> *(Revelation 21:1-3)*

"God himself will be with them." What a wonderful thought to warm my heart. Once in heaven there will be no more stormy days. No more cold windy days. No more lawns to care for. No more cold bodies.

The only thunderstorm we will hear is the thunder of His voice and the praise of His people saying, *"Praise the Lord! Salvation and glory and power belong to our God." (Revelation 19:1).* What a glorious spring day it will be when we find our home in the New Earth and the New Heaven!

Hard Stuff

What is your first reaction when a difficult situation comes your way? Do you bury your head in the sand and ignore the problem? When the hard stuff comes, do you forge forward with a plan? God gave us all unique personalities and therefore we react differently under stressful situations. Our spiritual walk also has a direct impact on our reaction to challenging situations.

I recently took on a new venture with my publisher. I have to admit I am excited, frustrated, worried, overwhelmed and just about any other adjective you would like to add to the list. Some pieces of this project are easy, while others, like creating videos, are quite challenging.

When it comes to challenges in my life, I am definitely a work in progress. There was a time when I would have walked away from a great opportunity saying, "No way!" The easy road with no stress involved was much more appealing. Today—this is hard stuff, but I look at the huge possibility of empowering more people for Jesus.

So how did I learn to face adversity rather than run from it? First of all, not all adversity is bad. God brings challenges into our lives as a means of growth. The harder the challenges, the more we need God. Thus, creating a circle: More faith leads to more growth. More growth leads to more faith.

Second, a whole lot of prayer. Prayer is the foundation I lean on during any situation. I didn't make the decision to jump into this venture without prayer, so how could I possibly conquer this gigantic project without Jesus? When I prayed about this undertaking, God answered with a resounding, "Yes!" Who am I to question God? I can only partner with Him to get the end result.

Queen Esther was challenged by the hard stuff in life. (I recommend you read the entire book of Esther, but I am going to focus on Chapters 3 and 4.)

The evil Haman disliked the Jewish people and convinced King Xerxes to issue a decree to destroy the Jewish people. When the Jewish people learned of their demise, they went into mourning. Queen Esther sent Hathach, one of the king's eunuchs, to see what was troubling her uncle Mordecai. Mordecai showed Hathach the decree, and directed Esther to go to the king and beg for mercy on behalf of the Jewish people.

Queen Esther was now faced her greatest challenge in life, requesting to see the king which actually put her life in danger. If he did not extend the gold scepter, she would be killed for coming to the inner court without his invitation. She expressed this concern to Mordecai.

> *Mordecai sent this reply to Esther. "Don't think for a moment that because you're in the palace you will escape when all other Jews are killed. If you keep quiet at a time like this, deliverance and relief for the Jews will arise from some other place, but you and your relatives will die. Who knows if perhaps you were made queen for just such a time as this?" (Esther 4:13-14)*

Mordecai's words convicted Queen Esther to put the lives of the Jewish people ahead of her own. She quickly decided to go to the king, but only after the Jewish people fasted and prayed with her for three days. During this time, God revealed a plan for Queen Esther on how to approach King Xerxes. In the end, she was successful. The evil Haman and his family were annihilated, and the Jewish people were saved and honored by the king.

Queen Esther didn't run and bury her head in the sand, she took the appropriate measures necessary to face the hard stuff in life. I am following Queen Esther's example and putting a plan in motion to conquer the hard stuff of this project. When you face difficulties in life, don't run and put your head in the sand. Forge ahead with a plan.

How to Face Hard Stuff

- Calculate the cost. Esther realized her life was at stake and evaluated the situation.
- Set priorities. It was more important to save the Jewish people than to save her own life.
- Prepare. Esther and the Jewish people fasted and prayed for three days.
- Course of action. She didn't wait for weeks or months to move forward, she put a plan in action after three days of prayer.
- Move ahead boldly. Esther's bravery is an example for us. Forge ahead and boldly face the Hard Stuff in your life.

Easy Stuff

We all face easy decisions in our lives. It could be as simple as what to fix for dinner, or which book to read next. (Thanks for choosing mine.) Those easy decision, will one day have an impact on a grander scale though. For example, allowing fast food to be your choice of dinner on a nightly basis will eventually lead to a bigger waistline. What you read has a direct impact on where you focus your daily thoughts. You can direct your mind toward God, or you can direct your thoughts toward some sort of filth. See how the easy stuff is just as important as the hard stuff in life?

Where we often lose our focus is thinking God doesn't care about the easy stuff, but He truly does. This is a Maryism here, but I truly believe this is where the verse *"Pray without ceasing," (1 Thessalonians 5:17)* comes into effect. We obviously cannot pray every minute of the day, or we would never accomplish any work. Praying nonstop, simply means to be mindful of God's presence at all times. When you and I are mindful of His presence, He is a part of all our decisions, which includes the easy stuff in life.

There is a short story tucked away in *2 Kings* 6, which seems so insignificant, you almost wonder why God included it. Yet it has a powerful message in a few verses.

Elisha had a school for prophets which was very prosperous. They had outgrown their meeting place and decided to build a larger facility. Elisha accompanied the men down by the Jordan river where they began to cut logs for the new school. Everything was going well until a man's ax head fell into the river. The man was concerned about losing the ax, because he had borrowed it.

As a prophet of God, Elisha knew this was easy stuff and there was no need to worry. He asked the man where the ax fell into the water.

> *"When he showed him the place, Elisha cut a stick and threw it there, and made the iron float. "Lift it out," he said. Then the man reached out his hand and took it."*
> *(2 Kings 6:6b-7 NIV)*

If you look at the big picture the ax is definitely easy stuff. Yes, it was borrowed but it wasn't a life-threatening event. There was no healing about to take place. No great battle to save the Israelites or lead them to the Promised Land. This miracle simply shows us that God truly cares about the easy stuff in life. Easy stuff, like losing a friend's ax head, or what to cook for dinner.

Nothing is too simple or too insignificant for our God. He cares about your dinner plans, and He cares which books you read. There is no problem too hard or too easy for our God. As you go about your day, be mindful of His presence and remember to always, *"Cast all your anxiety on him because he cares for you." (1 Peter 5:7 NIV).*

Dinner Table

My grandchildren Kennedy and Jackson are the politest three and four-year-old kids you will ever meet. I love hearing them say please and thank you, especially at the dinner table. They sound so grownup. It just makes me smile. They definitely have better manners than my boys had growing up. It isn't like Matt and Ryan threw food across the table at one another. But instead of hearing, "May I have more fruit please." It was more like, "Hey toss the Martian poop my way before you eat it all." (I will save Martian poop explanation for another devotional.)

Politeness is more of an attitude than it is the words please and thank you. One can speak without saying please and thank you, and still have an attitude of respect. Our good manners sometimes go by the wayside, simply due to anger, stress, and even pride. Arguments can ensue over what are unimportant circumstances considering the big picture. Believe it or not, rather than being polite to one another, the disciples argued at the Last Supper. I doubt they would have spent their last meal with Jesus quarreling, had they understood He was about to be crucified.

> *Then they began to argue among themselves about who would be the greatest among them. Jesus told them, "In this world the kings and great men lord it over their people, yet they are called 'friends of the people.' But among you it will be different. Those who are the greatest among you should take the lowest rank, and the leader should be like a servant. Who is more important, the one who sits at the table or the one who serves? The one who sits at the table, of course. But not here! For I am among you as one who serves." (Luke 22:24-27)*

To sit at the seat of honor was a status symbol during Biblical times, and quite often still is today. The disciples were shuffling, or should I say scuffling, for their rank with Jesus. All of their dinner table manners went by the wayside as they argued about who was the greatest among them.

Judas probably claimed that handling the finances was a huge responsibility, making him the greatest. Maybe John mentioned that he was Jesus' favorite disciple and closest friend. Peter probably reminded them of his ability to walk on water. They all had a claim to fame, and wanted to know who Jesus would select as the greatest among them.

Jesus reprimands them, and reminds them that Christianity isn't about a seat of honor, it is about serving others. He came to this earth as a man—not to be a king, but to be a servant. His entire ministry was based on serving others. Even during the Last Supper, He seized the moment to teach the disciples one last time to serve with love.

We are called to follow in Jesus' footsteps to serve others. Serving others comes in multiple ways. From teaching to shepherding. Administration to pastoring. Even young children, like Kennedy and Jackson, are called to have a servant's heart at the dinner table. They serve with respect, when they say please and thank you. In your daily life, remember what Jesus taught many years ago, *"Whoever wants to be a leader among you must be your servant, and whoever wants to be first among you must become your slave." (Matthew 20:26b-27).*

Oddities

As promised, here is the Martian poop story. Food develops strange names at the Rodman household. Martian Poop, aka Watergate Salad, was given the name by my husband. It was a favorite food at our home when the boys were growing up. It was fast and easy to make, plus it tastes great. I would often make it in the evening for the next day's supper. One day Jim said, "Hey the Martians came again last night. We get Martian poop for supper."

The reason for the name was the green color and the marshmallows. Marsh—Martian, Marshmallows—Poop. Get it? Jim loves to joke and have fun, and this was just another one of his antics which the boys enjoyed. Therefore, it will forever be called Martian Poop by the Rodman household.

Martian Poop became so common that when I passed the recipe on to my daughters-in-law, I actually wrote Martian Poop on the recipe cards because that is what Matt and Ryan would ask for. I guess we are an odd family giving our food such a strange name, but life is sometimes full of oddities. It can be the odd name given to a favorite dish, or it can be the odd way we treat others.

The Sadducees and Pharisees thought Jesus was an oddity too. His teachings to love unconditionally went against their strict rules and beliefs. They considered their enemies as enemies. Why would you ever love them? They found it very peculiar for Jesus to love someone, regardless of their race, their lack of wealth, their different nationality, or even their deformities. Even harder for them to comprehend was the fact that Jesus expected them to love others unconditionally as well. It went against every principal they were ever taught. In their belief system, you only loved those who loved you back.

> *"You have heard the law that says, 'Love your neighbor' and hate your enemy. But I say, love your enemies! Pray*

for those who persecute you! In that way, you will be acting as true children of your Father in heaven. For he gives his sunlight to both the evil and the good, and he sends rain on the just and the unjust alike. If you love only those who love you, what reward is there for that? Even corrupt tax collectors do that much. If you are kind only to your friends, how are you different from anyone else? Even pagans do that. But you are to be perfect, even as your Father in heaven is perfect." (Matthew 5:43-48)

Even today, it is often considered an oddity to follow the advice in this scripture. There are those who seem so unlovable. They challenge our Christian values to the core with their long list of idiosyncrasies. Yet we are called to love them in the name of Jesus. When we look at others through His eyes, we can't help but see their broken lives. They are no different than the woman caught in adultery, or the Samaritan woman in the scriptures. They are the ones who have been pushed away by society. The one's who need loving the most. The difference between then and now? Jesus isn't here to love the unlovable, but we are.

Martian Poop (Watergate Salad)

1 - 20 oz. can crushed pineapple with juice
1 - 3 oz. package of instant pistachio pudding
1 - 8 oz. carton of Cool Whip, thawed
1 to 1 ½ cups miniature marshmallows

Fold together all ingredients. Refrigerate several hours or overnight. Share with others in the name of love.

Adversity

Adversity is a common word for our lives. We simply cannot avoid difficulties in life. Sometimes they come in minor doses, and other times we have major difficulties to overcome.

My friend Leah battles OI, osteogenesis imperfecta, which is genetic disorder affecting the bones. This is a major adversity in her life, yet she is one of the most hopeful people I have ever met. For the past year, the side effects of the disease have been overwhelming. Everything from multiple broken bones, to heart problems, all a result of her OI. She has been in the hospital numerous times, has an unending list of doctor appointments, and a regimen of necessary medications each day. Adversity could easily be her middle name, yet she perseveres. Her human nature is to be fearful of what lies ahead, but her spirit is forever hopeful as she relies on the Lord for strength.

I thought of Leah today when I listened to my *Minute with Maxwell*. Today John Maxwell spoke about strength during difficulties in life. His final words were, "It's not what happens to you. It's what happens in you. Choose not to surrender to the adversity in your life." It was an ah-ha moment for me. Our attitude toward adversity is a choice! We are always going to face troubles, but we don't have to surrender to them. With God's help, we can overcome all of our difficulties.

Our adversities in life often bring us closer to God. I don't believe God causes the trials himself, but I do believe He allows us to walk through difficulties for a reason. The Psalmists often wrote about adversity, and how our magnificent God gave them strength during their times of need. The writer of *Psalm 66* undoubtedly had suffered and overcome a great deal of pain in his life.

Our lives are in his hands,
and he keeps our feet from stumbling.
You have tested us, O God;
you have purified us like silver.
You captured us in your net
and laid the burden of slavery on our backs.
Then you put a leader over us.
We went through fire and flood,
but you brought us to a place of great abundance.
(Psalm 66:9-12)

Regardless of the difficulties in her life, Leah does not surrender to them. She has been through battles and purified like silver, but she does not surrender. The slavery she experiences is the inability to function a normal life without pain, but she does not surrender. She has been through the fire and flood of procedures, but she has not surrendered.

The only time Leah has ever surrendered is to the Great Physician, because He hears her every prayer. Every prayer she says before surgeries and procedures. Every prayer she says when she is in pain. She continually prays for the strength for one more day on this journey, and God listens.

But God did listen!
He paid attention to my prayer.
Praise God, who did not ignore my prayer
or withdraw his unfailing love from me.
(Psalm 66:19-20)

I have learned from both the Psalmist and my dear friend to never surrender in the face of adversity. We only need to surrender to the Almighty Father who holds our lives in His hands.

Paradise

Picture in your mind a beautiful view which you consider paradise. For many it is a picturesque sunset over the ocean with the sound of the waves to relax them. Though I have enjoyed many beautiful ocean sunsets, my favorite view of paradise does not include an ocean. It is the view from my front porch.

After a long day of work, there is nothing more rewarding than sitting on the front porch and watching a beautiful summer sunset. The smell of the country air. The sound of the birds and possibly the flickering of lightning. The brilliant colors of the sky, as they fade from the yellow, into pink, orange and red. Then they fade into the gray-blue of the evening sky. I am so blessed by what God has given me that I am whisked away to paradise.

Here on earth paradise is what you envision. Paradise in a new earth and a new heaven will be quite different on day. There will be beauty which we cannot begin to imagine. A magnificent city built of pure gold with twelve beautiful inlaid stones of jasper, sapphire, agate, emerald, onyx, topaz, amethyst and more. The twelve gates to the city will each be made of one solid pearl. *"And the city has no need of sun or moon, for the glory of God illuminates the city, and the Lamb is its light." (Revelation 21:23).*

The new heaven will far exceed any glimpse of paradise here on this earth. On our most difficult days we long for paradise, but we desire our version of paradise. A place where we feel no pain and no turmoil. A place where we can simply relax and rest.

There will come a time with no more pain and no more work. No more stress and no more worry. No more evil practices, or dishonestly. No more long days and sleepless nights.

> *For the throne of God and of the Lamb will be there, and his servants will worship him. And they will see his face, and his name will be written on their foreheads. And there*

will be no night there—no need for lamps or sun—for the Lord God will shine on them. And they will reign forever and ever. (Revelation 22:3b-5)

But only those whose names are written in the Lamb's Book of Life (Revelation 21:27b) will be able to enter. Don't miss the opportunity to worship God the Father and the Lamb for eternity. Is your name is written in God's Book of Life? Please ask Jesus for the forgiveness of your sins by praying the prayer below, or your own salvation prayer.

Father,

You have blessed us with so many opportunities to see the beauty you have created on this earth. Beauty which seems like paradise to us. Yet it is nothing compared to the magnificent picture of heaven you gave us in the Bible. On our most difficult days here on this earth, may we always remember what glorious exquisiteness is yet to come.

I believe Jesus died, rose again and ascended to heaven that I might be forgiven of my many sins. I understand grace is a free gift which I cannot earn, but a gift to one day walk on the streets of gold by simply placing my faith and trust in you. Lord, please forgive me of my sins. Wipe them away, and give me a new heart. Give me the faith to understand that my name is now written in the Book of Life.

I praise You now and forever longing for the day I walk the streets of gold and sing, "Worthy is the Lamb who was slaughtered— to receive power and riches and wisdom and strength and honor and glory and blessing." (Revelation 5:12).

Amen

Suggested Scripture

- Revelation 21 & 22

Be Inspired

My publisher, Diane, has truly become my dear friend. Jim calls her my "paid friend," because I obviously pay her for publishing services. After working together for over a year, we are much more than associates. For us, every accomplishment is a reason to celebrate, no matter how big or small the hurdle. Don't misunderstand me and think all we do is celebrate, because we work hard. We have conquered difficult projects together, but somewhere in the midst of our busyness we cut loose and have a good laugh.

Over the weekend, I had great concerns about the direction of our current project. I feared it wasn't headed down a Christian path, which concerned me immensely. I wasn't on Diane's schedule to work together, but regardless she made the time. I shared my concerns and she was so understanding. The situation was instantly resolved and she thanked me for my input, and for holding her accountable to the Christian values she desires for Legacy Lane Publishing. As is typical with us, one conversation led to another. We continued to work on a couple of side projects, and enjoyed a great deal of laughter.

I am so blessed to have this type of relationship with my publisher. I called with the weight of the world on my shoulders, and a couple of hours later I was ready to tackle the world, one problem at a time.

Diane truly inspires me with every conversation! Interestingly, she feels the same way about me. She is not only a wonderful mentor, she is a magnificent friend. We are committed to one another through thick and thin. Within her publishing company, she is committed to Christian values and helping Christians get their messages out into the world. Within my books, I am committed to sharing God's Word in a simple, yet profound way, so others can understand and relate the scriptures to their lives. God has joined us together to help spread the Word, each in our own unique way.

Our commitment is similar to that of the first church of Thessalonica. Paul started the church, but soon fled for his life. Over the next couple of years, the church was under great persecution, but they stood firm in their beliefs. In his letter to the Thessalonians, Paul commends these young Christians for standing strong in the face of adversity.

> *We always thank God for all of you and continually mention you in our prayers. We remember before our God and Father your work produced by faith, your labor prompted by love, and your endurance inspired by hope in our Lord Jesus Christ. (1 Thessalonians 1:2-3 NIV)*

Doing God's work can sometimes carry a heavy load, but these young Christians persevered. How and why did they persevere? Their work was a product of their faith. Their labor was one of love. Their endurance was inspired. Inspired by their hope in the Lord Jesus Christ.

The work Diane and I accomplish together is parallel. Our work is a product of our faith. Our labor is one of love. Love for one another and love for the Lord. Our endurance is inspired. Inspired by our commitment to one another and our hope in the Lord Jesus Christ. My friend Diane truly has the gift of inspiration as she guides authors through the publishing and marketing process. I thank her from the bottom of my heart for the blessing she is to me.

Inspiration is so crucial in this difficult world. There are friends who come in and out of our lives. Cling tightly to those who inspire you to do great work for the kingdom of God, because inspiration will change the world one piece at a time.

Action Step

- Who inspires you in your faith?
- Let them know how much their inspiration fuels your passion for Jesus. Send a letter, an email, or give them a hug in person. Just let them know how valuable their gift of inspiration is to you.

Harmony

For the past few days, I have been staring at my plant across the room. I have never seen this happen before, but I guess it is going to bloom. There are no flowers yet, but a lot of tiny buds. What intrigues me the most are the tiny droplets in each crevice where the buds connect to the stem. The droplets never seem to go away or even run down the stem. Curiosity got the best of me and I stuck my finger into a droplet. I was shocked to discover it was very sticky and gooey. How odd, but if the plant was outside maybe that is what attracts bugs, ants, and bees.

You have most likely read enough of my devotions by now to know my next step. What does the Bible say about droplets, or gooey substances? At first I wasn't having much luck, but sometimes you just have to get creative in your search. I changed the word droplet to dew, and found this perfect scripture today!

How wonderful and pleasant it is
when brothers live together in harmony!
For harmony is as precious as the anointing oil
that was poured over Aaron's head,
that ran down his beard
and onto the border of his robe.
Harmony is as refreshing as the dew from Mount Hermon
that falls on the mountains of Zion.
And there the Lord has pronounced his blessing,
even life everlasting.
(Psalm 133 Emphasis added)

Sometimes we long for harmony in our lives. Disgruntled family issues. Discord in the church. Intense fellowship in our marriages. Unrest in the office. When one or all of these issues arise, harmony begins to dissolve. Then what? Well you can be like me—stick your finger into the sticky, gooey, droplet, or you can go to the Lord with your problems and seek a peaceful solution.

God longs for us to live in harmony with others. When there is harmony in the home, there is love. If the church has harmony, you will find an outpouring of love into the community. If you want productivity in the workplace, find harmony. Yes—life can be a sticky gooey mess, but don't allow your sticky gooey mess attract the unwanted bugs, ants and bees in your life.

Seek harmony with God and harmony in your life will surely follow.

> *Above all, clothe yourselves with love, which binds us all together in perfect harmony. (Colossians 3:14)*

Suggested Scripture

- Romans 12:16
- Romans 14:19
- Romans 15:5
- 2 Corinthians 13:11

April Snow

It is snowing in the middle of April! Yes, that is life in Ohio. The daffodils have bloomed. The maple trees are full of buds. The birds were singing. But today it is 32° F and snowing. I miss the cheery song of the birds this morning. Apparently, they are nestled down in their nests weathering the storm.

I love the seasons in Ohio, and even the quick temperature changes day to day. It is a good reminder that change happens, whether it is good or bad. (Or should I say "weather" it is good or bad?) You definitely learn to take advantage of the good days, because you don't know what tomorrow will bring.

Our Ohio days are like life—enjoy the good days, because you never know what tomorrow will bring. What does enjoying the good days look like for you? Some love to nestle into a good book with a cup of coffee. Others relax by watching their favorite movie for the fiftieth time. For many an outside activity to observe nature or bask in the sunshine makes a great day. For my shivering birds burrowed in their nests, a good day is fluttering about and singing.

The important part of the good days is to renew your soul. Life can be like an April snowstorm, so take advantage of those sunny days and build your faith. You can do all of the things you love in life to rejuvenate, but remember to include God on the journey.

The greatest rejuvenation we receive is meeting God where we are. Let me explain how to meet God while walking, reading or even watching TV with a few examples.

I love to walk outdoors. The fresh air and the exercise are great ways to clear my thoughts. When I take God with me by listening to Christian music, I replace the negativity in my mind with praise. It renews my soul.

Everyone in my family will tell you "Pretty Woman" is my favorite movie. I have watched it more than fifty times, probably more like a bazillion. Why do I love this movie? When Edward rescues Vivian from her life of prostitution, I have an image of God rescuing me from a world of sin. I don't just watch the movie, I watch the movie with God in my heart and on my mind.

The last book which captivated me was "Saving Stacy." It is a true story about a mass murder and the corruption within the sheriff's department to cover up the crime. I found myself having so much empathy for the only survivor, Stacy. I took God with me on this journey through many prayers for her. To be the only surviving member of such a horrific crime had to be devastating.

Regardless of how you enjoy your good days, remember to renew your soul. Give yourself the boost you need to make it through those difficult days. Spend some time with God and stay in His Word daily because verses like these, may be the lift you need to weather the storm.

> *When doubts filled my mind, your comfort gave me renewed hope and cheer. (Psalm 94:19)*

> *And be sure of this: I am with you always, even to the end of the age. (Matthew 28:20b)*

> *But I trust in your unfailing love. I will rejoice because you have rescued me. (Psalm 13:5)*

> *Devote yourselves to prayer with an alert mind and a thankful heart. (Colossians 4:2)*

The Relay Race

My son Ryan sent me a video of his two oldest kids having a relay race with an egg in a spoon. I have watched the video multiple times. I absolutely love how their personalities shine through their actions.

Jackson is our methodical, cautious, can't fail grandson. He had two hands on the spoon, his eyes on the egg, and walking only as fast as he thought possible so he wouldn't drop the egg.

Kennedy's motto could easily be—life is meant to be lived. She had one hand on the spoon walking as fast as she could. There was an occasional hesitation in her step to regain balance of the egg, but she was definitely on a mission to be the first one to her bucket.

On my video clip, Kennedy won by about two steps, but there were still more eggs to gather. I wonder if her not so cautious approach cost her the race in the long run. I never asked who won the race, because it wasn't about being a winner. It was about enjoying life and playing together.

Personalities. God definitely made all of us different. Part of our personality traits come from our mother and part from our father. The rest we develop over time ourselves. Jackson is four and Kennedy is not quite three. Already we see their differences, each one shines in their own unique way. I love how God made each of us special and unique with different passions in life. If we were all the same, can you imagine how boring life would be?

Did you ever wonder about Jesus' personality? Did He have some special charisma which attracted so many followers. Obviously, the Pharisees and Sadducees didn't like His persona and didn't believe He was the Savior. He challenged their behaviors to the core. No one was ever supposed to question their rules.

Jesus had so many followers He often had to retreat to quiet places of solitude. These three different versions of the Bible use slightly different words to describe Jesus' character.

> *No one has ever seen God, but the **one and only Son**, who is himself God and is in closest relationship with the Father, has made him known.*
> *(John 1:18 NIV Emphasis added)*

> *This **one-of-a-kind God-Expression**, who exists at the very heart of the Father, has made him plain as day.*
> *(John 1:18 MSG Emphasis added)*

> *No one has ever seen God. But the **unique One**, who is himself God, is near to the Father's heart. He has revealed God to us. (John 1:18 NLT Emphasis added)*

One and only Son. One-of-a-kind God Expression. Unique One. Every version has its own way of explaining that Jesus is different. He has to be different. He is God! If He were like anyone else, how would we know that He truly is the Savior of the world?

This wonderful God of ours created us in His image, but each of us has our own unique personality. Our children and grandchildren possess similar traits which have been passed down, but they also have their own individual personalities that set them apart.

The Sadducees and Pharisees couldn't put Jesus into their mold of rules and regulations. Likewise, we should not force children to fit into our mold for their lives. We need to nurture the uniqueness God gave them and allow them to grow, explore, create and thrive.

I cannot wait to see what Jackson and Kennedy will one day accomplish, because God has a plan for their lives. As they grow, I hope they understand their own unique personalities and say to God, *"Thank you for making me so wonderfully complex! Your workmanship is marvelous—how well I know it."*
(Psalm 139:14).

Mary Rodman

Social Distancing

Social distancing may date this devotional, but unfortunately it is part of our lives at this time. The lessons we learn during this time, are lessons we can apply to our lives forever.

The COVID-19 virus shut down this country and most of the world forcing us to stay away from one another. Many of us didn't realize how communal we were, until we were told not to gather at all. There was no lack of work at home, which made it easier, but I missed my church and my church family as the days ran together. God created us to fellowship with one another and to fellowship with Him.

Sometimes we can't remember what the preacher said on Monday morning (sorry Pastor Doug), but it is calming and peaceful to sit in the house of the Lord.

Fortunately, social distancing could not keep us from fellowshipping with God through prayer. Many set aside extra time to pray for their friends, and their family. We prayed for our leaders and our country and even our enemies. Many prayers were said, requesting that we be able to return to our churches soon. There is no end to the prayers we prayed through those weeks of distancing ourselves from others.

More than once the Israelites were exiled or unable to worship as they desired. After a period of longing to be in God's presence, they were once again able to return to Jerusalem. For the Israelites, the great city of Jerusalem was their place of worship, just as the church is for us today. In this Psalm, they expressed their joy when they are able to return to the great city and be in the presence of the Lord.

I was glad when they said to me,
"Let us go to the house of the Lord."

Pray for peace in Jerusalem.
May all who love this city prosper.
O Jerusalem, may there be peace within your walls
and prosperity in your palaces.
For the sake of my family and friends, I will say,
"May you have peace."
For the sake of the house of the Lord our God,
I will seek what is best for you, O Jerusalem.
(Psalm 122:1, 6-9)

Eventually, we too rejoiced when we are able to return to our normal lives. We hugged our friends, returned to work at the office, and we especially celebrated when we returned to our churches. Remember the lessons God taught you during this difficult time in our country. The importance of friends, family and employment. The significance of leaders, first responders and teachers. The blessing of good health. May you always remember the greatest lessons of all—freedom to attend church on Sunday and the power of prayer.

Grain Bin Construction

We are building a new grain bin on the farm. If you aren't familiar with farming, the bins are used for grain storage, allowing us to dry and store our grain directly from the field. This is a big project as the bin will hold 65,000 bushels of corn or soybeans. The diameter of the grain bin is 48 feet and it is approximately 55 feet tall. This bin is secured to a concrete pad which is about 2 feet above the ground, not to mention the concrete below the ground which we cannot see.

I give you these dimensions, simply so you understand the size of the project, and the work involved. The location for the grain bin was first selected and the site prepared for the concrete. Once the concrete was poured, it had to cure for about a week, before the construction of the grain bin could start.

Grain bin assembly begins with the roof. Each day rings are added to the bottom, as the crew lifts it higher and higher, until completed and anchored to the foundation. The ladder, the strengtheners for support, and a safety platform on top are all assembled at the appropriate stages and attached during the process.

The construction of the grain bin is similar to the construction of our walk with Christ. We start with the prep work when Jesus calls us into a relationship with Him. Once our heart is prepared, we allow Jesus to be the Lord of our life. *"So now we can rejoice in our wonderful new relationship with God because our Lord Jesus Christ has made us friends of God."*
(Romans 5:11).

Next comes the foundation on which we stand. That 2-foot-deep slab on concrete, resembles God our Rock. *"No one is holy like the Lord! There is no one besides you; there is no Rock like our God." (1 Samuel 2:2).* We begin to understand the unfailing love of God. His infinite capabilities, and His all-knowing ways. His unshakable love for us becomes the foundation on which we build our lives.

The assembly of the grain bin roof appears to be a tedious process. The work crew closely follows an instruction manual as they carefully construct it. Your roof is Jesus, who provides protection from the evil one. *"But the Lord is faithful; he will strengthen you and guard you from the evil one." (2 Thessalonians 3:3).* Your instruction manual is the Bible. There is no greater manual, than the one written by God himself. *"For the word of God is alive and powerful. It is sharper than the sharpest two-edged sword, cutting between soul and spirit, between joint and marrow. It exposes our innermost thoughts and desires." (Hebrews 4:12).*

Your ladder, your strengtheners for support, and your safety platform are all the wonderful ways you stay connected to Jesus. Prayer, meditation, and study. They are continually added at the appropriate times in your life. The good times and the bad. Times of celebration and loss. During laughter and tears. In all of these situations, you need a ladder of prayer to reach Jesus. Your strengtheners are a time of reflection and meditation as you renew your spirit. The Word of God is definitely your safety platform where you are always able to turn to the scriptures for strength, for hope and for celebration.

Your grain bin is your life, and it too is a big project. Don't allow your grain bin to collapse or your foundation to crumble over time. Use your ladder of prayer without ceasing. Remember your strengtheners are reflection and daily meditation. Stand upon your safety platform, the Bible, to maintain an impeccable relationship with Jesus.

The Skunk

The last couple of years we have battled various critters living underneath our deck. Everything from ground hogs to skunks, and trust me the skunk was quite a concern. We finally caught him in the live trap, but Jim was unable to take him out because he hurt his back.

He looked at me and I quickly exclaimed, "No way, not me!"

Jim's brother George came to my rescue and got the skunk. I gave him an old blanket which he used to cover the trap. He loaded the trap with the skunk into the back of his pickup truck, and off they went. I don't know where he took the skunk, but anywhere except my house was fine with me.

It is spring, and all those critters are looking for homes again. I don't want them under my deck, so I built a barrier around the bottom with paver bricks. I hope this makes it more difficult to dig and they go elsewhere. I'm doing my best to deter all critters, and especially the skunk!

After the Israelites settled in the Promised Land, the Jordan River was a barrier between the tribes. Moses gave the tribes of Reuben, Gad and the half-tribe of Manasseh land on the east side of the Jordan, while the remaining Israelites settled on the west side.

After the battles for the Promised Land ended, Joshua called together all of those who possessed land on the east side of the Jordan River. He thanked them for their obedience to fight in the battles. He blessed them, and sent them on their way back to their homeland across the river.

Before the tribes of Reuben, Gad and the half-tribe of Manasseh crossed the river, they stopped and built a large altar which resembled the Temple of God. The remaining tribes were upset about the altar, because they thought the tribes on the east side of the Jordan were mocking God. They were prepared to attack in the name of the Lord, but since they had been through so many battles together, they decided to send a delegate of men to talk first. The tribes who built the altar meant no offense to God or the remaining tribes of Israel, and graciously explained why they built the altar.

> *"The truth is, we have built this altar because we fear that in the future your descendants will say to ours, 'What right do you have to worship the Lord, the God of Israel? The Lord has placed the Jordan River as a barrier between our people and you people of Reuben and Gad. You have no claim to the Lord.' ...So we decided to build the altar, not for burnt offerings or sacrifices, but as a memorial. It will remind our descendants and your descendants that we, too, have the right to worship the Lord at his sanctuary with our burnt offerings, sacrifices, and peace offerings. Then your descendants will not be able to say to ours, 'You have no claim to the Lord.'" (Joshua 22:24-27)*

The tribes on the east side of the river didn't want the barrier of the Jordan River to ever separate them from the rest of the Israelite nation, or keep them from worshipping God. The situation was quite the opposite of what the others thought. The altar was simply a memorial which would serve as a reminder of their unity with one another, and their faith in God.

Even though the Jordan River served as a barrier between the tribes, the Israelites solved their worries peacefully that day. I created my own barrier between me and the many critters who lived under my deck. They are part of God's creation, and I too am looking for a peaceful resolution. They just need to live on their own side of the "Jordan River" and we will get along just fine.

I don't want my memorial to be the day I was sprayed by a skunk on my deck. I want it to be my faith and the lessons God taught me over the years.

What memorial can you leave for your family which represents a strong faith in the One true God?

Suggested Scripture

- *Joshua 22*

Adulterous Woman

Did you ever put yourself in the position of the woman caught in adultery? *(John 8:1-11).* She was suddenly dragged out into public and cast down at the feet of Jesus. The shame and humiliation she experienced had to seem almost unbearable. The Pharisees didn't care about her sins. If that were the case, both her and the man should have been stoned to death. *(Deuteronomy 22:22).*

The Pharisees were simply using her in a game to trap Jesus. Jewish people were not permitted to carry out their own executions, so if Jesus said to kill the woman, they would report Him to the Romans. If Jesus said not to kill her, He was breaking the law of Moses. All they cared about was proving Jesus wrong.

I envision this woman on the ground, curled up in a ball, trying to cover herself as people stared at her. Possibly she had tears streaming down her face with her arms over her head as she cowered in fear. There she was, all of her emotions bubbling out, as she was put on public display and humiliated.

The scriptures don't tell us about her fear, her shame, or her humiliation. Was she brokenhearted enough to cry out to God? She is about to receive the hand of grace, but at this point in the story she doesn't know what her future holds. Are the stones about to hit her body, or will this man they call Jesus rescue her?

This is what I call a "Maryism" because I have no biblical proof to back up my assumption. I wonder if she prayed and asked God to spare her life. If Jesus is about to extend the hand of grace, He had to know what was in her heart! She may not have known Jesus was the son of God, but she had hit rock bottom (no pun intended) with only one place left to turn—God.

We sometimes allow ourselves to hit rock bottom before we reach out to the Lord. Oh, the unnecessary emotions, agony, and shame we carry, rather than seeking comfort from God's

Word. *Psalm 69* has wonderful words for all the emotions the adulterous woman felt. These words of comfort will bless our lives also. Don't go through life with a broken spirit. When you face difficulties, turn to this wonderful Psalm written by the psalmist David. Carry these words in your heart as a reminder that God is close to the brokenhearted.

Below is just a glimpse at some of the wonderful words of *Psalm 69*. We will never know if the Adulterous Woman cried out to God, but we do know: *"Jesus stood up again and said to the woman, 'Where are your accusers? Didn't even one of them condemn you?' 'No, Lord,' she said. And Jesus said, 'Neither do I. Go and sin no more.'" (John 8:10-11).*

In just a few short moments, her accusers walked away and Jesus offered her the hand of grace. What an amazing story of redemption for all of us who feel condemned by our sinful life!

> ***Sin & Hatred*** *"I am the favorite topic of town gossip and all the drunks sing about me. But I keep praying to you, Lord, hoping this time you will show me favor. In your unfailing love, O God answer my prayer with your sure salvation. Rescue me from the mud; don't let me sink any deeper! Save me from those who hate me, and pull me from these deep waters. Rescue me from the mud; don't let me sink any deeper! Save me from those who hate me, and pull me from these deep waters." (Psalm 69:12-14)*

> ***Shame*** *"You know of my shame, scorn, and disgrace. You see all that my enemies are doing. Their insults have broken my heart, and I am in despair. If only one person would show some pity; if only one would turn and comfort me." (Psalm 69:19-20)*

> ***Pain & Suffering*** *"I am suffering and in pain. Rescue me, O God, by your saving power." (Psalm 69:29)*

For a deeper look into the lessons you can glean from the Adulterous Woman, purchase ***Cast the First Stone be Transformed by Grace*** at www.MaryRodman.com/Books.

Pine Trees

This spring we removed seventeen pine trees from our yard. For several years we have battled bagworms, so most of the trees were dying and a few others were removed due to bad locations. We still have plenty of trees, but it looks so barren where two large clusters of pine trees once edged our driveway. One of those groups was outside my office window. I loved to gaze at the birds as they flew in and out of the trees. I found it relaxing, and I really miss viewing nature from my office chair.

I felt a little guilty as the trees toppled that day. Many birds lost their homes, and had to rebuild their nest elsewhere. There are still numerous pine trees which provide a dense cover of protection for them. I miss watching the birds, but change is good and God gave them the resilience to move to new locations.

Just as my birds suddenly faced great difficulties, the disciples were about to endure great troubles on the night Jesus was betrayed. They were accustomed to walking with Christ daily, following His teachings, and His directions. He had served as their protection against evil, and now their world was going to be turned upside down when Jesus is arrested.

Jesus knows what they will face after He is taken away, and in those last few moments of freedom, He still has a servant's heart. His unfailing love for His disciples and for the future believers resonates in His heart as He prays for unity of the believers and God's protection over them.

> *I pray for them. I am not praying for the world, but for those you have given me, for they are yours. I will remain in the world no longer, but they are still in the world, and I am coming to you. Holy Father,* ***protect them by the power of your name****, the name you gave me, so that they*

may be one as we are one. My prayer is not that you take them out of the world but that you protect them from the evil one. My prayer is not for them alone. I pray also for those who will believe in me through their message. (John 17:9, 11, 15, 20 NIV Emphasis added)

"*Protect them by the power of your name.*" I wonder if the disciples truly understood the importance of these words Jesus prayed that fateful night. Do we understand them ourselves? It is remarkable that on His final days, or maybe even His final hours, Christ put the needs of others first. Yes, Jesus prayed for himself, but in the midst of His turmoil, He asked God to protect the disciples and the future believers.

Praying for someone who does not exist is a hard concept for us to understand, but not for an all-knowing God. To Him we already existed. He knew us by name. He knew the turmoil, the evil ways, and struggles we would face. The most important act of love He could share on His final days was to request God's protection over us through prayer.

In all my visions of Christ's final hours, as He poured out His heart and soul to God, I never envisioned Him praying for me. Little ole, crazy, country girl me. I am totally blown away by the love of Jesus.

A week ago, I was concerned about the birds losing their protection in the pine trees. Before I ever existed, Jesus was concerned about protecting me from the evil one. Can we even fathom His love for us this side of heaven? Just before he was arrested, Christ prayed and expressed that His greatest desire was for us, the future believers, to know and love God our Father, the Mighty Protector.

> *"O righteous Father, the world doesn't know you, but I do; and these disciples know you sent me. I have revealed you to them, and I will continue to do so. Then your love for me will be in them, and I will be in them."*
> *(John 17:25-26)*

Suggested Scripture

- *John 17*

Mary Rodman

The Uncles

A dear friend of mine recently shared how she knew two of my uncles. Both of them assisted her and her husband on the remodeling of their old farm house. She remembers their kindness, helpfulness, and how they endlessly gave of themselves.

Uncle Dick was a very gifted and talented carpenter. He could tackle any remodeling or building project with great skill. The harder the project, the more he seemed to enjoy it. After retirement, he continued to make beautiful woodworking projects for special people in his life. He made my mother countless items, including a beautiful inlaid end table and knickknack shelves from the wooden arms of my Great Uncle Joe's favorite chair.

Uncle Chuck owned a backhoe business. He also was not afraid to tackle any project. Even though he was hard working, I remember him as the uncle who made life fun. He had a special way of making everyone feel loved and important.

As a child, I remember sitting on his semi-trailer at our house. Just Uncle Chuck, our dog Duke, and myself. Uncle Chuck began to tickle me, which made Duke jump on me and get in my face. Giggling and squirming I meant to say, "Uncle Chuck stop," but it came out as "Uncle Duke stop!" From that day on, Uncle Chuck always reminded me his name was now Uncle Duke. I was the only person allowed to call him Uncle Duke, which made me feel even more special.

I treasure memories from my childhood, but even more important is remembering the people. The generations ahead of us taught important life lessons. The importance of hard work, and perseverance on a job. The value of sharing your gifts and talents with others, whether it is your profession, or your hobby. One of the greatest lesson we can ever share from our ancestors is how to make others feel special and loved.

Mary, the sister of Martha and Lazarus, loved Jesus with all her heart. She knew Jesus was the Savior. A man who loved unconditionally, taught endlessly, and healed the lame. She always had a heart of worship when it came to Jesus. From sitting at His feet to learn, to anointing His body with expensive perfume, Mary always showed compassion for her Savior.

Near the end of His ministry, Jesus was in Bethany at the home of Simon. When Mary entered the home, she broke the jar of expensive perfume from essence of nard and poured it over Jesus head. Many of the attendees complained about Mary wasting the perfume. Judas Iscariot even reprimanded her for wasting expensive perfume. He claimed the perfume could be sold, and the money used to feed the poor, even though he had no intentions of doing so. Jesus quickly defended Mary's actions, because He understood Mary's heart and her act of worship.

> *"Leave her alone," said Jesus. "Why are you bothering her? She has done a beautiful thing to me. The poor you will always have with you, and you can help them any time you want. But you will not always have me. She did what she could. She poured perfume on my body beforehand to prepare for my burial. Truly I tell you, wherever the gospel is preached throughout the world, what she has done will also be told, in memory of her."*
> *(Mark 14:6-9 NIV)*

Jesus' last few words in this scripture are so powerful. *"What she has done will also be told, in memory of her."* What a wonderful reminder to share the memories of those who have been our teachers and mentors in life. We had the privilege of learning from them, so we need to continually share their memories with future generations.

I challenge you to share a memory of someone who made you feel special as a child, or taught you a great life lesson during your life. Not only will you honor their memory, you will pass on the knowledge you gained, and inspire other people.

Knight in Shining Armor

Many years ago, when the boys arose one morning, Jim was tossing items out of the closet by our back door. He had seen a mouse, and he was on a mission to get him.

In the midst of the turmoil, Matt announced there was a bat on a spindle of the staircase. I was quick to tell Matt there was not a bat in the house, and he immediately showed me the BAT! I promptly told Jim to forget about the mouse and go get the bat!

Trust me, this was not a typical morning at the Rodman household, just one with a little extra excitement. I don't remember if Jim caught his mouse that day or later, but we never had a mouse problem. Bats however were a different story. It was quite some time before we were able to stop them from getting into our house. They were so frequent that Jim kept his bat-fighting-arsenal gear outside our bedroom door. A badminton racquet, an empty jar with a lid, and a pillowcase.

Let me explain the procedure. When a bat was in the house, Oreo, our tiny house cat would chase it. Her commotion and running around would wake me. I would scream, "Bat!" and dive under the covers. (Did I mention just how much I hate bats?) Jim would put on his gear and go in for the battle.

The pillowcase went over his head, because he hated the bat swooping toward his hair. His weapon of choice was the racquet to bring the little culprit down. Once the bat was down, I would fetch the jar and he would put it in the jar to take it outside. Can I just say, Oreo definitely earned her keep over the years, and I have not missed the bats since we moved! I know God created all creatures for a purpose, but those little critters need to stay outside. They are just plain scary when they swoop around in the house.

As I was writing this story, I chuckled at the sight of Jim with his pillowcase over his head and his racquet in hand as he went in to fight bats. It has been so many years, but I still envision my knight in shining armor coming to my rescue in a time of need.

There is one knight in shining armor that is even greater than my hubby, and His name is Jesus. No one can ever replace Him in my heart.

God defends me. *"Father to the fatherless, defender of widows—this is God, whose dwelling is holy." (Psalm 68:5).*

God protects me. *"But let us who live in the light be clearheaded, protected by the armor of faith and love, and wearing as our helmet the confidence of our salvation." (1 Thessalonians 5:8).*

God fights for me. *"What shall we say about such wonderful things as these? If God is for us, who can ever be against us?" (Romans 8:31).*

God rescues me. *"For he has rescued us from the kingdom of darkness and transferred us into the Kingdom of his dear Son, who purchased our freedom and forgave our sins." (Colossians 1:13-14).*

If I had not been too nervous and scared to pray, God would have even saved me from the bats lurking in the middle of the night. However, I am forever thankful for my knight in shining armor on earth, who came to my rescue on multiple occasion to bring down the bats.

Rock Bottom

I have a friend who after several years, still feels the pain of an unwanted divorce. When we occasionally bump into one another, I try to offer words of encouragement and remind him that he is a great person. When we part ways, I pray he will find peace and happiness again soon.

In essence, he questions how other Christians can be so hurtful. His ex-wife, who is a Christian, left him for someone else, leaving a huge hole in his heart. I know bad things happen to good people, and good things happen to bad people. That is just life. I also understand that we are all human, and even Christians make decisions which seem to be against their beliefs from time to time. From the outside looking in, I question her motives, but only God knows why this happened.

My motto has always been that God never wastes anything in our lives. He takes both our bad and good moments and uses them for His glory. God often uses these bad painful situations to get our attention. As it is often said, "When you hit rock bottom there is only one place to turn, and that is to Jesus."

So, when you hit rock bottom, how do you ever find a way out of the pit? In this painful situation, my friend has to start with forgiveness. If we don't allow ourselves to forgive, we will become bitter and bitterness eats at your soul. *"Watch out that no poisonous root of bitterness grows up to trouble you." (Hebrews 12:15b).*

We also have to understand and believe that God feels your pain. *"The Lord hears his people when they call to him for help. He rescues them from all their troubles. The Lord is close to the brokenhearted; he rescues those whose spirits are crushed. (Psalm 34:17-18).*

Jesus is patiently waiting for you to reach out to Him for comfort. For many that is a walk through the woods, or enjoying

God's beautiful creation. Some immediately turn to God's Word, especially the Psalms, for comfort. Others find comfort in music and the arts. Wherever you feel God's presence, know that He is there to heal your broken heart.

Ask God to heal your broken heart and give your life new purpose and meaning. The New Testament if full of examples where Jesus healed the physical bodies of others, but He also healed their emotional burdens.

One example is the woman who touched the hem of Jesus garment. *(Luke 8:43-48)*. Due to her constant bleeding, she was considered unclean by Jewish laws. Can you imagine the emotional burden she was carrying because she was an outcast person? Her faith in Jesus healed her that day. Jesus healed her physically, and He healed her broken heart.

This woman had faith—we need to have faith—is there really any difference? It is our faith in Jesus which brings us total healing from hurtful situations. When we believe in Him, and put our trust in Him we begin to experience a new life.

> *The fundamental fact of existence is that this trust in God, this faith, is the firm foundation under everything that makes life worth living. It's our handle on what we can't see. (Hebrews 11:1 MSG)*

Faith is the foundation on which we build our relationship with the Savior. We can't begin to understand all the benefits of a strong faith. He is capable of much more than we can comprehend, from physical healings, to the emotional support He provides. What I do understand is that with every step of faith we take, He reaches out to save us.

I pray that if you have hit rock bottom, you will take a step of faith and reach out to the One who hears your desperate cries for help. He will lift you out of the pit of despair, and set your feet on firm ground once again.

Grandfather May I

By the time I was old enough to remember Grandpa Conklin, he was bedridden. Regardless of his condition, I have fond memories of him playing "Grandfather May I" from his bed. Like most old houses, each room had multiple doors allowing you to circle through many rooms. My sister Janet and I started at his bedside and he sent us out the door into the living room. We would battle our way across the room, circle through the dining room, and back down the short hallway into his bedroom through the other door. All the while fighting for who would get to Grandpa first for a prize, which was usually a piece of candy.

In the excitement, we would often forget to say, "Grandfather may I" and have to return and start over. The most exciting part of the game was the home stretch. As I child, we were sure Grandpa didn't know who was winning as we headed down the short hallway out of his sight. He obviously knew, and always remembered who won the last time to make it even. Grandpa chose to make life fun for us and himself, in spite of his difficulties.

I came across this little quote today, which reminded me of Grandpa. *"Don't wait for everything to be perfect before you decide to enjoy your life." ~Joyce Meyer.*[ii] Grandma and Grandpa certainly didn't have a perfect life, but they had a joyous one. They lived in a house which wasn't fancy, but it was more than adequate to meet their needs. I don't remember them having an abundance of money, but enough to survive. Grandpa obviously dealt with health issues and Grandma took care of him for many years. What I remember the most are the fun times. Playing "Grandfather May I" was the perfect example of enjoying life with their grandkids.

Jesus doesn't expect you and I to live perfect lives either. Obviously, it is impossible to do so. It is our attitude in life which allows us to experience great joy in the midst of this imperfect world. We need to set our sights on our heavenly rewards to find pure joy here on earth.

> *"Do not let your hearts be troubled. You believe in God; believe also in me. My Father's house has many rooms; if that were not so, would I have told you that I am going there to prepare a place for you? And if I go and prepare a place for you, I will come back and take you to be with me that you also may be where I am." (John 14:1-3 NIV)*

What beautiful words Jesus spoke to the disciples as He prepared them for the days to come. Jesus' death and resurrection soon followed, but beforehand He assured the disciples not to worry about their struggles in life here on earth.

Our troubles, imperfections, and struggles will always exist here on earth, but when we fix our eyes on the Savior, He gives us joy in the midst of the chaos in life. So, step away from the turmoil, and play a game of "Jesus May I." Pray for perfect peace and joy from Him, as you focus on the beauty of heaven, which is yet to come!

> *"You will keep in perfect peace all who trust in you, all whose thoughts are fixed on you!" (Isaiah 26:3)*

Ryan Jr.

Our grandson, Jackson, is a spitting image of his dad. So much that I often refer to him as Ryan Jr. He worries about little things like his dad. He especially loves tractors, trains, and planes like Daddy does. We often have the pleasure of smiling and saying, "Payback time," whenever Jackson does something to annoy his father.

On one of their recent stops at our house, I grabbed Jackson's hand to lead him from the barn to the porch to talk to Grandpa. Ryan however hopped in the truck and drove to the house. Jackson instantly began to worry.

"What is Daddy doing? Where is he going? I don't understand why Daddy isn't coming to the porch?"

In just a few seconds, Jackson was filled with worry and curiosity, which gave me a chuckle because I remember those days well. I assured him that Daddy was coming to the porch too. No matter how much I tried to reassure Jackson, he never took his eyes off of his dad the entire time.

As Jackson grows he will hopefully worry a little less, but I hope he never takes his eyes off of his father, because Ryan is a great daddy. The best way for Jackson to learn, is to focus on the example in front of him.

Likewise, the best way for us to learn is to keep our eyes focused on Jesus. The acronym, WWJD—What Would Jesus Do, is sometimes overused, but it is also great advice. When we pause, and consider this question, it often keeps us from making bad decisions, or saying words which we cannot undo. What are some of the lessons we can learn by following Jesus more closely and digging into God's Word?

Patience *"May God, who gives this patience and encouragement, help you live in complete harmony with each other, as is fitting for followers of Christ Jesus." (Romans 15:5)*

Compassion *"When he saw the crowds, he had compassion on them because they were confused and helpless, like sheep without a shepherd." (Matthew 9:36)*

Love *"But anyone who does not love does not know God, for God is love." (1 John 4:8)*

Endurance *"We do this by keeping our eyes on Jesus, the champion who initiates and perfects our faith. Because of the joy awaiting him, he endured the cross, disregarding its shame. Now he is seated in the place of honor beside God's throne."*
(Hebrews 12:2)

Those are just a few of the qualities of Jesus which we should strive to achieve, but there are so many more. Each day we walk with the Lord, brings us that much closer to having a heart like Jesus to serve others.

Points to Ponder

- Look for scriptures which describe the characteristics of Jesus by using the concordance in your Bible, or an online source such as www.Biblegateway.com.
- Some ideas: Forgiveness, Faith, Joy, Peace

Jackson, our Ryan Jr., almost 5 years old

Recipe for a Happy Life

It is the little things in life that make a huge difference in our hearts. A hug from a child, a spouse, or a friend. Settling in with a good book in the morning sunshine. A few quiet moments with God in the middle of the day. Sometimes it is showering your friends with an unexpected homemade treat.

When life gets super busy, we often miss the moments of splendor, which seem insignificant in the day-to-day struggles. We forget to look at the flowers in bloom, or to take an evening walk. On the rainy days we sulk, instead of anticipating the rainbow which is about to emerge when the sunshine returns.

Our lives can be in turmoil, or even under construction as God pulls at our heart strings to make a change, to see Him more, or to be with Him more. In those moments, look for the small blessings which surround you!

Listen to the birds in the morning sun. Read a good book. Journal your thoughts. Thank God for the blessings in your life, which you have not previously acknowledged. Most importantly—watch for the rainbow following the storm, because it is a symbol that God will always keep His promises.

Your rainbow may not be a physical rainbow in the sky, but a moment in time which makes you smile. All too often we miss these golden opportunities in life. These are the moments which lift our spirits and make life beautiful.

If you are surrounded by troubles, or having a humdrum day, search for God, and bask in His presence. It doesn't have to be an earth-shattering moment to acknowledge His existence. He is everywhere, all the time, simply waiting for you to say hello.

O God, you are my God;

I earnestly search for you.
My soul thirsts for you;
my whole body longs for you
in this parched and weary land
where there is no water.
(Psalm 63:1)

Life Gets Sticky

Last night I dropped an entire gallon of sweet tea on the kitchen floor. The plastic jug cracked and tea spewed all over the cabinets, the floor, and me. I was cooking supper at the time, and had food which needed my attention. I turned the burners off on the stove, and requested Jim's immediate assistance. He tossed me some towels, flipped the asparagus in the air fryer and mumbled something like "I don't know what else to do," and returned to the living room. I guess it was out of his realm to assist me with the kitchen disaster, but for me it was just another day because I drop items all the time.

I threw the towels into the tea puddles, mopped up the mess and put the towels in the washing machine. I finished prepping supper, and the food turned out just fine. I can't say that I enjoyed my meal, as I knew a sticky gooey mess was awaiting my attention. I quickly gobbled down my supper and returned with a bucket of soapy water to clean the cabinets and the floor.

It definitely was not my plan to clean and mop the kitchen at 7 PM, but it happens. Sometimes life just gets sticky. You have to learn to go with the flow, even when the flow is a gallon of sweet tea. How we react to the unexpected overflows in our lives is what makes a difference. We can act like a raving lunatic, flapping our arms and yelling, or we can mop up our messes.

Was I upset, of course. Did I rant and rave? Not that I remember, but maybe you should ask Jim his opinion.

I have been around those who choose to rant and rave as their tempers flare, which only makes the problem bigger. It is much less stressful for everyone involved to simple say, "oh well it happens," and tackle the situation.

James warns us about controlling our tongues, and reminds us that praising Jesus and cursing should not come out of the same mouth. (*James 3:9-10*). It isn't always cursing that fuels the flame, it can be a good rant that changes the atmosphere and makes those around us want to crawl in a hole and hide.

> *Indeed, we all make many mistakes. For if we could control our tongues, we would be perfect and could also control ourselves in every other way. The tongue is a small thing that makes grand speeches. But a tiny spark can set a great forest on fire. And among all the parts of the body, the tongue is a flame of fire. It is a whole world of wickedness, corrupting your entire body. It can set your whole life on fire, for it is set on fire by hell itself.*
> *(James 3:2,5-6)*

Our speech can be uplifting, or it can be hurtful. When life gets sticky, we all too often speak before we should. I am reminded of Jesus braiding a whip before He cleared the temple. We also need to braid a rope before we speak during sticky moments. (*John 2:15*).

How many hurtful words would go unsaid, if we simply said a quick prayer (while braiding a rope) during sticky situations in life?

Natural Gift

Have you ever thought about what natural gift you possess? Some people know and use their gifts continually, while others are oblivious to the possibility of a gift which naturally impacts others.

Reflecting on my days of working full-time in an office environment, a few people come to mind. Deb's natural gift was a contagious smile. It didn't matter how stressful, how gloomy, or how blah her day was, she wore a smile. She was a constant reminder to everyone to put on a happy face and enjoy life.

Cindy on the other hand had a contagious laugh. She could start a giggle fest in a matter of minutes, and probably over something others didn't even find humorous, but we all joined in.

Laurinda was the encourager in the office. She saw the good in everyone and as the receptionist had contact with so many people each day. She showered her positive words to visitors and employees on a daily basis.

My friend Dee is a hugger! You are not going to visit her without receiving a hug. And my husband, Jim, loves to leave everyone with a joke at the end of a conversation. His goal is to brighten someone's day with a little humor.

I have friends and family who always end conversations with, "I love you," or "I appreciate you." Once again, a natural gift from God. Words that easily flow from their lips to lift someone's spirit.

If you don't know your natural gift, don't compare yourself to others, because that will just make it more confusing. I don't have a contagious smile or laugh. You probably won't hear me say, "I love you," at the end of the conversation, and you definitely won't hear me tell a joke because I never remember them correctly. My strongest natural gift is friendliness. Even in elementary school, teachers pulled me aside and asked me to take new students under my wing and help them make friends.

God blessed each of us with a special natural gift. It is up to us to recognize, develop, and use it to its full potential. As you contemplate my closing question, keep these two Bible verses in mind, because God made you unique and special for a purpose in this world.

> *I praise you because I am fearfully and wonderfully made; your works are wonderful, I know that full well. (Psalm 139:14 NIV)*

> *Many are the plans in a person's heart, but it is the Lord's purpose that prevails. (Proverbs 19:21 NIV)*

What natural gift do you possess and use to make others feel loved and special?

My Joke

Okay, I do know one joke I can share with you.

What did the fish say when he hit the cement wall?
Dam.

The Golden Girls

On the farm, we are in our busy season of combining wheat and baling straw, which means I am in the kitchen cooking most of the day. Rather than having humdrum days of endless cooking and dirty dishes, I decided to watch some of my favorite sitcoms on the iPad while I work. After all, it is a proven fact that smiling and laughter release endorphins which are good for the body and soul. So why not laugh while I work, it will certainly help keep me going!

My all-time favorite sitcom is *The Golden Girls*. Each episode has humor, life lessons, hugs, tears and more humor. All too often I see myself or my friends in one of the characters, which makes me laugh even harder. While watching an episode the other day, I jotted down this quote to share with you.

> *"The older you get, the better you get—unless you're a banana." Rose, The Golden Girls*

Praise the Lord I'm not a banana that is beginning to rot. I do however believe life gets better as we age. We may get a little slower, but we also get a little wiser. I am busy all the time, yet I feel more fulfilled than I did in my younger days. My "retirement careers" of helping on the farm, babysitting grandkids when needed, and writing books have all been wonderful blessings. God continually teaches me lessons each day, even when I'm watching *The Golden Girls*.

> *But the godly will flourish like palm trees and grow strong like the cedars of Lebanon. Even in old age they will still produce fruit; they will remain vital and green. They will*

declare, "The Lord is just! He is my rock! There is no evil in him!" (Psalm 92:12,14-15)

I love the words in this Psalm. They are a beautiful reminder that we are never too old to produce fruit for the kingdom of God. For those of us who have reached the "Over 60 Club," we have wisdom to share with the younger generation. Just because we rise a little slower, and life sometimes moves at a snail's pace, it doesn't mean that we are useless. God has given us a life full of experiences to share with family and friends. Part of that wisdom is the importance of a smile and laughter.

I recently put together a list of my books for a friend. I realized that in four years, I have published two devotionals, two matching journals and two Bible studies. Granted that was just before I hit the "Over 60 Club," but that is a lot work for this aging lady. The best part is the smiles and laughter as I walk down memory lane and share my stories.

Don't allow your age, or your boring, routine life pass you by—life if meant to be lived. Remember we are never too old to smile, laugh, or produce fruit for the kingdom of God.

So, what are you waiting for? Go enjoy the day, put on a smile, create some laughter, and share your wisdom!

Baling Crew

Wheat season and baling straw for 2020 is complete. What a whirlwind it has been the last couple of weeks. I was blessed with kitchen help this year and I am thankful for Cindy's assistance. I'm not sure I could have cooked all those meals by myself. I'm not getting any younger, and the crew isn't getting any smaller. It takes a lot of planning, shopping, cooking, and stamina to feed 8-10 people two meals a day for two or three weeks.

Every baling season comes with its typical mini storms. Spilled food (in the kitchen and the field). Men caught in the pouring rain. Equipment breakdowns. Not enough manpower. Bad directions to the next field, and sometimes bad decision due to the unpredictable weather. All of these issues coupled with long hours and short nights make for a long two-week stint of hard work.

We have two young men who help every year. I call them the Young Bucks. They are full of energy and consume mass quantities of food. The remainder of the crew is part of the over 60 crowd, who I refer to as the Old Guys. (Retired farmers never really retire, they just work for someone else from time to time.) We all work together as a team, which lightens the burden for everyone.

In *Acts 27*, Paul also worked as part of a team on the ship which set sail for Rome. The crew and prisoners onboard had their share of storms. These weren't mini storms like we face baling straw, these storms were life threatening as their ship was tossed around on the open sea. Paul was one of the Old Guys on the ship, and even though he was a prisoner, he was respected by the commanding officer. Paul offered advice and encouragement to the crew as the ship battled the storm.

> *Paul called the crew together and said, "... None of you will lose your lives, even though the ship will go down. For last night an angel of the God to whom I belong and whom I serve stood beside me, and he said, 'Don't be afraid, Paul, for you will surely stand trial before Caesar! What's more, God in his goodness has granted safety to everyone sailing with you.' So take courage! For I believe God. It will be just as he said." (Acts 27:21-25)*

I love how Paul seized the moment in the midst of a storm and shared about God. He encouraged them to put their faith in the One true God. Paul also broke the bread, gave thanks and began to eat. He begged the crew join him as they had not eaten in almost two weeks. Everyone soon followed and ate some much-needed nourishment. Eventually, they were shipwrecked on the island of Malta, but as promised, God spared the lives of everyone onboard.

While reading this chapter, *Acts 27:38* jumped off the page at me, like a metaphor. *"After eating, the crew lightened the ship further by throwing the cargo of wheat overboard."* Our baling crew lightens their load by supporting one another and enjoying moments of laughter as they gather for food.

We too can throw our cargo of stress and worry overboard, and lighten our load by giving them to the One true God.

Jigsaw Puzzle

Our lives are much like a giant jigsaw puzzle. The many pieces make up who we are, where we have been, and our plans for the future. All of the intricate pieces of our lives work together to create a unique person designed by God.

A jigsaw puzzle has a distinctive border, but God's desire is for us to stretch our borders. Many live within their borders, never searching beyond for other possibilities. They are content to live inside their comfort zone. Others push the limits and strive to continually expand their borders. They start out a 300-piece puzzle, but over time expand their boundaries to 500 pieces. Growth continues, and they become 1000 pieces and more! They don't grow overnight, because expanding their borders requires hard work, perseverance, and courage.

When you put together a jigsaw puzzle, you focus on the color, the shape, and the size of each piece. Slowly, all of the pieces come into focus and a picture emerges.

The most important step to assemble the puzzle pieces of your life is to focus on God. He will lead you every step of the way, as the pieces fall into place. Just like the jigsaw puzzle, slowly a great picture emerges. When you walk with God, the possibilities for your future are endless.

After wandering in the wilderness for years and years, the Israelites were about to expand their borders. God told Moses that he would not cross the Jordan River and enter the Promised Land with the Israelites. Before they parted ways, Moses challenged them to: *"Be strong and courageous." (Deuteronomy 31:6).*

He then repeated those same words directly to Joshua, because Joshua was about to assume the role of leadership for the Israelites. Joshua's number of puzzle pieces and his border were about to be expanded greatly.

Then Moses called for Joshua, and as all Israel watched, he said to him, "Be strong and courageous! For you will lead these people into the land that the Lord swore to their ancestors he would give them. You are the one who will divide it among them as their grants of land. Do not be afraid or discouraged, for the Lord will personally go ahead of you. He will be with you; he will neither fail you nor abandon you." (Deuteronomy 31:7-8)

What a huge responsibility! The Israelites were rebellious people, and Moses even predicts that they will rebel again after his death. Joshua had assisted Moses every step of the way, but now he was leading them into battle for the Promised Land. Joshua didn't question his new responsibilities or turn from them. He faced them with great confidence, knowing the Lord would fight the battles for the Israelites. Joshua expanded his border and walked confidently with the Lord as they crossed the Jordan River without Moses.

Are you as brave as Joshua? What is your Jordan River? Don't fear the unknown, instead walk by faith and follow Christ. He will lead you across the Jordan River into the Promised Land as He multiplies your puzzle pieces of life. You will find great blessings when you allow God to put all of the intricate pieces of your life together and continually expand your border.

Leave Egypt

Seldom do I remember my dreams, but recently I was awakened by a nightmare. I don't recall many details, which is a good thing, but I do remember there were flies involved. Lots and lots of flies and it was making me squirm!

The flies in my dream remind me of the plagues God brought upon Egypt. How did the they cope with all the disasters? There was no water to drink because God turned it into blood. Then came the frogs hopping and jumping everywhere. Gnats—pesky little gnats swarming around your face and around your house.

Next were the FLIES! I envision them crawling on everything and flying everywhere. They probably had to cover their faces and swing their arms just to walk. If those flies were anything like the ones in my dream, I would have helped the Israelites pack their belongings, load their camels, and joined the crowd to escape.

That was just the beginning of the plagues and Pharaoh still refused to let the Israelites leave. God continued to bring His wrath upon Pharaoh and the Egyptians. He killed their livestock, and gave the animals and the people horrible boils. He sent hail and locusts which destroyed the crops, and the people who refused to seek shelter. He sent darkness for three days. It was so dark they could not even see one another.

Throughout each of these plagues Pharaoh's heart remained hardened, which God predicted before Moses ever left Midian for Egypt. *(Exodus 4:21).*

> *But the Lord hardened Pharaoh's heart, and just as the Lord had predicted to Moses, Pharaoh refused to listen. (Exodus 9:12)*

There are numerous accounts in the book of Exodus similar to the verse above. Reading these passages reminds me of many debates about free will versus God's destiny. It is a difficult subject to wrap your head around, but I love how the footnote in my study Bible addresses this question.

> *"God gave Pharaoh many opportunities to heed Moses' warning. But finally God seemed to say, 'All right, Pharaoh, have it your way.' And Pharaoh's heart became permanently hardened. Did God intentionally harden Pharaoh's heart and overrule his free will? No, he simply confirmed that Pharaoh freely chose a life of resisting God. Similarly, after a lifetime of resisting God, you may find it impossible to turn to him. Don't wait until just the* ***right*** *time before turning to God. Do it now while you still have a chance. If you continually ignore God's voice, eventually you will be unable to hear it at all."*[iii]

God sent His final blow when all of the firstborn sons of Egypt died. The firstborn males of the livestock. The firstborn sons of the lowly maid servants. And the firstborn son of Pharaoh. Finally, Pharaoh demanded that the Israelites leave Egypt. *(Exodus 12:31-33).*

God knows what is in our hearts and whether we will resist Him or run to Him. Don't wait for the final blow to turn to God. Leave behind what holds you captive. Run from the frogs, the gnats, and the flies. Leave behind the darkness and all the other plagues in your life. Don't wait for the final blow to turn to God. Leave behind what holds you captive. As you leave Egypt and turn toward the Promised Land, allow God to soften your heart!

At the Heart of It

At the Heart of It was a contest sponsored by Beck's Hybrids. Beck's is the company which we purchase our seed for the farm. The contest instructions were very simple. Do something creative to explain what is *At the Heart of It* for you as a farm family. My granddaughters decorated their papers with sequins, markers and stickers. After much thought, I decided to enter the contest as well. I tossed around several ideas and settled in on a poem.

I chose to include this poem as a devotional for you. Though it is based around farm life, please focus on the idea *At the Heart of It*. In other words, why do you do the things you do? Why do you go the extra mile at work? Why do you help the needy or give financially to others? We serve others in many ways, but what is important is why we serve.

At the Heart of It

We plant the corn, the beans, and the wheat.
We work all day in the cold and the heat.

Some farmers raise hogs, cattle, and sheep
Others grow veggies and berries so sweet.

We work like mechanics and wait for spring thaws.
We tackle odd jobs. Bale the hay and the straw.

Farming's a lifestyle, where we enrich others.
Serving beside both sisters and brothers.

Why do we work so hard in the dust?

Feeding God's people—it is a must!

You ask what's at the heart of it all?
Listening to God and answering His call.

Few are destined to serve in this way,
But here on the farm generations may stay.

The poor widow woman understood exactly what was *At the Heart of It*. She didn't give because she had to. She gave because she wanted to. *"For they have given a tiny part of their surplus, but she, poor as she is, has given everything she has." (Luke 21:4).*

How about you, what is *At the Heart of It*? Is your "why" for accolades and praise, or is your "why" centered around a heart for Jesus?

Something out of Nothing

Like many of you, there was a time in my life when I experienced a season of grief. In a period of about five years, I lost four family members. Following the loss of my brother-in-law and sister-in-law, life was different, but it seemed to move forward. Dad and Mom always taught us to pull ourselves up by the bootstraps when difficulties arise, and so I did.

When the third devastating loss hit our family, those bootstraps no longer worked for me. The loss of my sister Linda sent me into a season of grief. A pain which I was not accustomed to and did not know how to handle.

I was thirteen years younger than Linda, so my childhood memories of her are far and few between. I always joked and said, "I left for kindergarten and Linda left for college."

However, as adults we enjoyed heart to heart sister talks on a variety of subjects. In the final months of her life we spent a great deal of time together, because I provided transportation to many of her doctor appointments. Our sister bond was growing closer each week, and then the Lord called her home.

The holidays were quickly approaching, and I was dreading it. How could we possibly gather for a family Christmas and pretend that everything was normal? You see, Linda was the life of the party with her boisterous voice and contagious laugh. You could hear her tell a story and cackle from two rooms away.

I had countless talks with God, begging Him to remove my pain and replace it with wonderful memories of my sister. The moment I realized I could not overcome my broken heart alone, life began to change for me. God took my nothing—the worthless pain of grief, and turned it into something—joyful memories of Linda.

Grief is a difficult time in our lives, and we all deal with it differently. For me, I began to make Christmas ornaments out of Linda's old handkerchiefs. The moment I made something—Christmas ornaments. Out of nothing—Linda's old handkerchiefs, joy began to fill my heart. God brought healing into my life through those ornaments. Whenever I gave one away, I shared a fond memory about her and said, "This was one of Linda's handkerchiefs."

Walking through the loss of my sister impacted me greatly. I'm not saying the worthless pain of grief is nothing, because it is a true pain. An ache in your heart which sometimes seems unbearable. What I am saying is that grief does nothing to help you move on with your life. You need to take the next step by changing your daily or weekly routine.

God did a great healing in my life that Christmas. Mom passed away less than two years later, and the grief process was much easier for me this time. I understood that I was not walking the path of grief alone. Christ was with me every step of the way.

We read numerous stories of Jesus healing the lame and the blind. Those same wonderful stories of healing can be applied to our broken hearts.

> *Then they reached Jericho, and as Jesus and his disciples left town, a large crowd followed him. A blind beggar named Bartimaeus (son of Timaeus) was sitting beside the road. When Bartimaeus heard that Jesus of Nazareth was nearby, he began to shout, "Jesus, Son of David, have mercy on me!"*
>
> *"Be quiet!" many of the people yelled at him.*
>
> *But he only shouted louder, "Son of David, have mercy on me!"*
>
> *When Jesus heard him, he stopped and said, "Tell him to come here."*

So they called the blind man. "Cheer up," they said. "Come on, he's calling you!"

Bartimaeus threw aside his coat, jumped up, and came to Jesus. "What do you want me to do for you?" Jesus asked.

"My Rabbi," the blind man said, "I want to see!"

And Jesus said to him, "Go, for your faith has healed you." Instantly the man could see, and he followed Jesus down the road. (Mark 10:46-52)

Jesus is still in the healing business today. Like Bartimeaus, we need to call out to Him and say, "Son of David have mercy on me! My heart is breaking."

When Bartimeaus called out for help, Jesus asked him, "What do you want me to do for you?"

The moment Bartimeaus replied, "I want to see!" Jesus healed him.

Jesus is asking you, "What do you want me to do for you?"

What is your reply? Will you ask Him to remove your grief, and heal your broken heart? Maybe you simply need to ask Christ to show you how to make something out of nothing. You do not have to make Christmas ornaments to turn your broken heart into joy. Your healing may come from sharing your grief story, singing your favorite music, or becoming more involved in your church or community.

If you are in a season of grief, God has given you the ability to move forward with your life. Call out to Him and say, *"Son of David, have mercy on me!"* He is waiting for you to make a change and turn in a new direction. He will meet you where you are, in the midst of your sorrow, and show you how to make something out of nothing.

Devastation in Iowa

I have always said that farming strengthens our faith. We can plant the best seed, and use all the newest farming practices, but we have no control over the weather.

My heart breaks for my fellow farmers in Iowa this week. I have seen many pictures of the devastation they experienced following horrific windstorms. Some of the farmer's grain bins were destroyed. Their tall beautiful corn has now been flattened to the ground just weeks before harvest. Even some of the grain elevators experienced severe damage. The farmers and grain elevators both have less storage available with harvest quickly approaching. I wonder if the farmers will have a corn crop to harvest, and if so, where will they possibly store or sell their grain.

In central Ohio, we have experienced some drought conditions in some areas this year. Our drought now seems so trivial compared to the Iowa devastation. We are definitely not expecting a bumper crop, but we are blessed with crops to harvest and storage facilities to store the grain.

In difficult times such as these, it is easy to question God. We wonder why some suffer, while others have abundance. But in reality, the circumstances are not ours to question, because only God can send the rain, calm the storms, and control the winds.

Our earthly minds cannot fathom God's sovereignty in situations such as these. It is hard to comprehend that He is a just and fair God, and that all earthly happenings, both good and bad, occur for a reason. Regardless of our difficulties, who are we to question God during the trials in life.

Job also experienced the pain and agony of great losses in his life. He continually claimed his innocence of any wrongdoing against God. He questioned God's motives for stripping him of family, livestock, possessions and even his health.

Ultimately, Job humbled himself before God and said, *"You asked, 'Who is this that questions my wisdom with such ignorance?' It is I—and I was talking about things I knew nothing about, things far too wonderful for me." (Job 42:3).*

What a power packed verse! We love to justify our thoughts and actions when we are in the midst of trials in our lives. We find it much easier to justify our heart ache, than to trust in God's authority. God uses these wearisome moments to draw us closer to Him and to strengthen our faith.

Just like Job, we need to humble ourselves before the Almighty God. We live in a sinful world where both good and evil people suffer. The difference between the two, is putting your trust in God and understanding that your suffering will one day come to an end.

In the midst of the wind and storms in your life, wait patiently before God and put your trust in Him. Only God can bring the rain, calm the storms, and control the winds in your life. Remember He is still on the throne, and He is still in control.

Happy Place

Picture in your mind your happy place. For some it is a walk in the woods, a cabin in the mountains, or a stroll along the beach. Many people enjoy the morning silence with a cup of coffee in their favorite chair. Possibly it is the view from your front porch, or a leisurely drive in your car. Wherever your happy place is—go there in your mind.

I believe Peter's happy place was the Sea of Galilee. This is where Jesus first asked Peter to become a disciple, and where Peter committed to a lifetime of serving Jesus to build the Christian church.

Peter's journey began with Jesus walking along the shore of the Sea of Galilee. He calls out to Peter and Andrew who were casting their nets into the water, *"Come, follow me, and I will show you how to fish for people!" (Matthew 4:19).*

Jesus had preached in the area for several days, so Peter and Andrew already knew about Him. There was no hesitation, no doubt or fear. They immediately dropped their nets and followed Jesus.

Peter and the remaining disciples traveled with Jesus throughout His ministry. Peter watched as Jesus fed five thousand men with two fish and five loaves. He and the other disciples maneuvered Jesus through crowds of people who were seeking miracles and healings. Peter was the only disciple with enough faith to walk on water. A feat none of us would attempt today.

Jesus preached, healed, taught, showed compassion, and loved everyone. But not everyone liked Him. He was often in the midst of controversy with the Sadducees and the Pharisees because He challenged their manmade rules. It was because of these controversies that Peter feared for his life and denied Christ three times the night that Jesus was arrested.

Peter had his ups and downs as a disciple, but his love for Jesus continued to grow. In spite of both the good and the bad moments, he never regretted his decision to follow Jesus.

Three years after Peter became a disciple, Jesus was crucified and had risen from the dead. Before ascending to heaven, Jesus once again walks along the shores of Galilee. He sees the disciples fishing and calls out to them, but they do not recognize Him from the distance. Jesus seizes one last opportunity to teach the disciples by performing another miracle. He instructs them to toss their nets on the right-hand side of the boat, and immediately their nets were full and overflowing.

That day, Peter was doing what Peter loved—fishing on the Sea of Galilee. He was enjoying his happy place. Once they were ashore, Christ challenged Peter and asked him three times, "Do you love me?" Each time Jesus asked the question, He used a different Greek word for love. Essentially Jesus asked, "Do you love me? Do you really love me Are you even my friend?"[iv]

Each time Peter replied, *"You know that I love you." (John 21).*

Many scholars say Jesus challenged Peter three times, because Peter had denied Christ three times. Jesus was persistent because He wanted Peter to understand true grace. He didn't want Peter to dwell on his past mistakes, he wanted him to know he was truly forgiven.

Peter's life was never the same after that encounter on the shores of Galilee. Peter gave total control of his life to Christ, and God used him to build the Christian church. He went from being a fisherman, to being an evangelist. He knew from experience that the road ahead wouldn't be easy. There would be times of joy, and times of trial. He would need the Lord's strength for the journey, and rest in His peace on days of turmoil.

The greatest change in Peter's life was the moment he understood that Jesus alone is the true meaning of love. Three years prior he committed to being one of Jesus' disciples. But on this day, he made a lifetime commitment to follow Jesus wherever the road would lead.

So, are you still at your happy place in your mind? A place where you are calm, your troubles are few, and you have a peaceful smile on your face. You look off into the distance, and you see someone walking toward you, but you don't recognize Him. This man calls out to you, and suddenly you realize it is Jesus. You and Jesus are alone. He calms your fears as you relax in His presence. There is a radiance which seems to surround the two of you, then He lovingly asks, "Do you love me? Do you really love me? Are you even my friend?"

Jesus is longing to hear those same words Peter spoke so many years ago, *"Yes Lord, you know I love you."* Give Jesus total control of your life, because Jesus alone is love. He will take you places far beyond your happy place.

> *We know what real love is because Jesus gave up his life for us. So we also ought to give up our lives for our brothers and sisters. (1 John 3:16)*

The Poof

My oldest granddaughter Mya has been learning to make cookies by herself. She has all the measuring down to a science as she levels all of the cups and spoons properly. Yesterday, we worked on the proper order to add the ingredients, and how long to run mixer after each addition.

She was doing a great job and on the last step, so I turned my attention to her sister who needed help with her sand art. That is when I heard it. The big poof.

If you put too much flour in at once, or turn the mixer on too fast it poofs flour all over the place. In Mya's excitement of making her peanut butter cookies, she turned the mixer speed up about three notches, creating a small flour dust storm.

"Oops! Grandma, I forgot about the poof!"

I turned to see Mya brushing flour off of herself. She also had flour on the counter, and flour on the floor. Not to miss an opportunity for some fun, Mya realized that the flour on the floor allowed her to slide back and forth. As she began to roll her cookies and place them on the tray, she did a slip-slide dance back and forth across the floor. I however, quickly scurried for the broom and dustpan before the poof became an even bigger mess.

We experience a lot of poofs in a lifetime. There are those occasions when we appear to be covered in flour after an embarrassing moment. And there are the bigger poofs like shame or humiliation from big mistakes in our lives. We wonder—how could anyone love me? And worse yet, why would Jesus even care about me after so many mistakes in life?

The Samaritan Woman experienced the shame of a many poofs in her life. Not only was she a Samaritan which the Jews despised, she had a sorted past. She had been married five times and was not married to the man she was currently living with. *(John 4:17)*.

We don't know the details of these marriages, but obviously, it had an impact on her self-image. When Jesus asked her to go get her husband, she doesn't share any of her sorted details, she simply says, *"I don't have a husband." (John 4:17)*.

Jesus, who is all knowing, tells her about the past marriages in her life. This Jewish teacher not only came into Samaria which was unheard of, but He actually talked to her and knew all about her past. She was intrigued by Him, but was quick to change the conversation by asking Jesus questions.

There was something different about Jesus, but what was it? As the conversation continues, Jesus finally says to the her, *"I am the Messiah!" (John 4:26)*. Immediately, the Samaritan Woman believed that Jesus truly was the Messiah.

> *"Come and see a man who told me everything I ever did! Could he possibly be the Messiah?"* ***So the people came streaming from the village to see him.***
> *(John 4:29-30 Emphasis added.)*

Do you get it? It doesn't matter how many poofs (five marriages and a live-in-boyfriend) she had in her life. Christ scurried for His broom and dustpan and swept it all away with His amazing grace! When she shared her story with the people, they saw a woman who was converted. The Samaritan Woman once lived with shame and humiliation, but now she openly shared about Jesus all over town.

During this conversation with Jesus, she discovered grace and freedom from her past. She understood the truth about Him, and the truth set her free. She became a courageous witness for Jesus.

The Samaritan Woman experienced a great deal of transformation through a heart to heart conversation with Jesus. Don't be burdened by the shame and humiliation of the poofs in your life. Spend a few moments with Jesus and discover the same wonderful life changing grace she experienced.

The Samaritan Woman's greatest change was the hope which only Jesus can give. You too can experience this life changing hope by taking all of your poofs in life to the Lord.

> *For I fully expect and hope that I will never be ashamed, but that I will continue to be bold for Christ, as I have been in the past. And I trust that my life will bring honor to Christ, whether I live or die. (Philippians 1:20)*

Mya age 8 as she continues her baking skills.

The Dirt Patches

Earlier this year we removed numerous pine trees from our yard. It was not a good time to plant grass seed, so I simply mowed the weeds all summer. In addition to planting grass, we were also eliminating a flowerbed. September is here and it is time to plant the grass seed. Oh, how I am dreading the work ahead of us.

First, we needed to kill the weeds, but that was the easy part. Jim sprayed the weed patches, and we left for vacation. We returned to brown patches in our yard, which was a reminder of the big job ahead of us. Jim repeatedly told me not to stress, which meant he had a plan. (I just love it when he has a plan better than mine.)

His plan included Ryan, a young man who helps us on the farm from time to time. Ryan ran the tractor, and the tiller. He picked up roots, rocks, landscaping bricks and clumps of weeds. As if that wasn't enough, when I began to move some of my ground cover plants, he pitched in and helped with that too.

Soon, two big patches of dirt were ready for grass seed. There is still work to do in other areas, but he will return tomorrow to help again. I feel so blessed to have his help.

Our lives are full of dirt patches—those little parts of our soul which need to be tilled and replanted. Often, we feel like we have to clean up our lives before we can allow Jesus to do the planting. That is so far from the truth. No matter our mistakes, stumbles, or battles, Jesus is there to help us overcome. We don't have to do the work, because Jesus already did at Calvary. Our only job is to accept His grace.

I love this passage in *Romans 5* which explains the difference between the law, which condemns us, and Jesus Christ, who sets us free.

God's law was given so that all people could see how sinful they were. But as people sinned more and more, God's wonderful grace became more abundant. So just as sin ruled over all people and brought them to death, now God's wonderful grace rules instead, giving us right standing with God and resulting in eternal life through Jesus Christ our Lord. (Romans 5:20-21)

Sin entered the world when Adam and Eve sinned in the garden of Eden. As a result, everyone has dirt patches in their lives. Sin is not something we can avoid, but grace covers our sins like new grass on a dirt patch. The dirt patches in our lives are filled with beauty because of God's grace.

Ryan helped me with the dirt patches in my yard and God helps us with the dirt patches in our lives. Stop focusing on the dirt in your life, and focus on God's grace. You don't have to do the hard work. You simply have to accept God's free gift of grace and allow Him to clean up your life.

I am looking forward to pretty green grass where the dirt patches once were. You too can enjoy your beautiful life because "he *will give a crown of beauty for ashes." (Isaiah 61:3).*

Work Hard & Enjoy Life

Losing a loved one is never easy, but it is part of life. Focusing on the memories, the lessons they taught us, and the blessings we received from them, helps us on those difficult days.

Two of my brothers-in-law, Tweety and Bumpy, went home to be with the Lord this year. They were from opposite sides of the family, and to my knowledge they didn't know one another. Not only did they have unusual nicknames, they were bigger than life itself. They were the type of people who lit up a room when they entered. Complete strangers were easily drawn into their circle, as they enjoyed life. Their jokes, pranks, and all around ornery personalities shined in all they did.

On the flip side, they had an incredible work ethic. They were hard working men, and always eager to lend a hand. Long after retirement, you would find them working on a project, driving a tractor, or helping a friend. It was just part of their DNA—that desire to stay busy and to do for others.

I discovered this Bible verse just a few days before Bumpy passed away. It was so fitting for him that I thought my concordance should actually have the word "Bumpy" with a reference to *Ecclesiastes 8:15*.

> *"So I recommend having fun, because there is nothing better for people in this world than to eat, drink, and enjoy life. That way they will experience some happiness along with all the hard work God gives them under the sun." (Ecclesiastes 8:15)*

This verse describes Bumpy, and it also describes people who impact our lives with their robust personalities and hard-working principles. We often wonder, "How do they have such a great attitude in life when I feel so drained of energy?"

There are moments when life's work seems endless and we long for a vacation, or just a break from the monotony. If that is how you feel, maybe you need to check your attitude. (I am preaching to the choir here, because I did an attitude check this morning.) It isn't the workload that is creating the problem, it is the outlook toward the work which causes the agony in our lives.

Solomon, a man known for his wisdom, had this figured out years and years ago, and yet many of us don't heed his advice. The key to enjoying life is a mixture of hard work, and enjoyment. That doesn't mean work for eight hours and then play the rest of the day. We need to mix the two together. In other words, "Whistle While You Work," like Snow White.

I know it is challenging to always enjoy life. It is a struggle for me because I can become overwhelmed easily. God's desire is for us to be so grounded in Him, that we can enjoy the hard work, the daily grind, the mundane, and yes, even the sad loss of a loved one. True enjoyment comes when we hold tight to the Savior in the midst of the storm, or during a heavy workload. That is when we truly see the Light on a bad day.

My favorite hillbilly, Tweety, will always hold a special place in my heart. I miss his greeting of, "How ya doin' hunny chil'." But I know when I get to heaven one day, he will greet me with his southern twang and invite me to the party.

God broke the mold when he created Bumps. I will always remember him as the Eveready Bunny. He never slowed down, unless it was to pull a prank, tell a joke, or have a good meal.

Thank you to my brothers-in-law who taught me to work hard, and enjoy life. One day, I too will be rejoicing in heaven with the Eveready Bunny and my Favorite Hillbilly. But before I leave, I want to leave a legacy of a person who enjoyed her life to the fullest, just like the example they set!

Legacy of Prayer

I am the laity speaker for our church service Sunday. Since I just wrote the previous devotional, *Work Hard & Enjoy Life*, my thoughts were immediately drawn to the legacy we leave behind as the sermon topic.

My brothers-in-law left behind a legacy of working hard and enjoying life. My mother-in-law's legacy was her caring spirit. She delivered produce from her garden, and homemade goodies to family, friends and neighbors for years.

Did you realize that the legacy of prayer is the greatest gift you can leave behind when you pass away? Yes—prayer. Even after we have gone on to be with the Lord, our prayers will continue to be answered.

We may not see the answers to our prayers in a timely manner. We have our timeframe and God has His. We only see the current moment, but God sees the greater picture and the greater good. He sees everything and will answer our prayers according to His will at the most opportune time.

Never before have I considered my prayers to be a legacy. Once I understood this to be true, it was a game changer in my attitude about praying. When we pray for others, it becomes part of our legacy, because long after we are gone, our prayers impact the lives of those we love.

A perfect example of this is Hannah, who we read about in *1 Samuel 1*. She desperately prayed for a son, to the point of anguish, she poured her heart out to God and said, *"O Lord of Heaven's Armies, if you will look upon my sorrow and answer my prayer and give me a son, then I will give him back to you.* ***He will be yours for his entire lifetime****, and as a sign that he has been dedicated to the Lord, his hair will never be cut."*
(1 Samuel 1:11 Emphasis added).

God granted her a son the following year, and she named him Samuel. When he was weaned, Hannah returned to the Tabernacle in Shiloh. Following their sacrifice, Hannah brought the boy to Eli and said, *"'I asked the Lord to give me this boy, and he has granted my request. Now I am giving him to the Lord, and he will belong to the Lord his whole life.' And they worshiped the Lord there." (1 Samuel 1:27-28).*

Samuel became one of the greatest men in the Old Testament and died at an old age. He was faithful to God his entire life, which fulfilled Hannah's prayer, *"He will be yours for his entire lifetime."*

How remarkable is this? The prayer Hannah prayed before Samuel was even conceived, lived on into Samuel's old age!

This shows that the greatest and most powerful legacy we can leave behind, is our prayers. They don't have to be long, flowery, perfect prayers, just prayers from our hearts.

I have been very convicted about the legacy of prayer this week, and I hope you will be too. There is no greater gift that we can leave behind, than the powerful prayers we say for others. Remember, God will answer your prayers, according to His will, in His time—even after we are singing with the angels in heaven.

Fear of Men

I recently shared with my Radiant Writer's Community friends about my fear of speaking in front of men. I was to speak at our church the following morning, and I was already getting nervous. Sue, our guest speaker for the day, said my fear most likely stemmed from my childhood, and shared an example.

After much thought, I recalled one teacher, Mr. X who found great pleasure in humiliating me when I was in middle school. It wasn't just one incident, but continually. Due to my complexion, I turned extremely red in gym class. He found it funny to poke my forehead with his finger, because it would change from red to white. All the while, drawing my classmate's attention. Humiliation #1, but not the root of the problem. I truly believe this next incident is where my fear of speaking in front of men stems from.

As a class, we had taken a fieldtrip and during the trip we were allowed to chew gum. Once we returned, we had only ten to fifteen minutes left in the day. I should have spit out my gum, but of course I forgot. Mr. X caught me chewing the gum, and he made me stand in front of the class with the gum on my nose. I was so humiliated and embarrassed that I almost passed out. One of my classmates saw me swaying and came to my rescue by getting Mr. X's attention. (I wish I knew who that was so I could thank them today.) Of course, almost passing out just added to the humiliation. He pointed out to the class that I couldn't even stand for ten minutes with gum on my nose.

Sadly, what Mr. X did to me, he also did to others. Sometimes much worse, especially when it involved girls. Our school system chose to move him to the high school, instead of reprimanding him for his actions. I wonder how many young people have unjustified fears because of his actions.

Once I began to understand my fear, God brought several references to my attention. I had just read these words in *Draw the Circle*, by Mark Batterson.

> *"All of us have a unique voiceprint, not just physically but spiritually as well. God wants to speak through you differently than through anyone else. Your life is a unique translation of Scripture.*[v]*"*

I have a unique message to deliver on Sunday morning, and Mr. X will not be at church. Once I realized where the fear was stemming from, my fear began to lift, but true healing was found in God's Word.

> *This is why I remind you to fan into flames the spiritual gift God gave you when I laid my hands on you. For God has not given us a spirit of fear and timidity, but of power, love, and self-discipline.* ***So never be ashamed to tell others about our Lord.***
> *(2 Timothy 1:6-8a Emphasis added).*

God has given me a voiceprint, and an audience which I am to reach. I cannot allow incidents from my childhood to keep me from speaking on His behalf, and neither should you. We should never be ashamed to talk about the Lord, because when we give in to our fear, Satan wins.

We can allow our past to rule our lives, or we can overcome our past with God's help. If something from your past is haunting you, conquer it in the name of Jesus, because you have a unique voiceprint, a message to share with the world, which only you can share.

Points to Ponder

- What fear from your past is impacting your current situations?
- Once you identify the source of your fear, find the appropriate scripture to overcome.
- What is your unique story about Jesus to share with the world?

Rearview Mirror

I was doing my usual grandma duty—the pickup line at school—when I saw one of the sweetest moments I have witnessed in quite some time.

It was almost time for the kids to be released, but too chilly to stand outside my car. So, I was watching in my rearview mirror for Mya and Reagan. My eyes were immediately drawn to the father and daughter in the car behind me. (Father and daughter to the best of my knowledge.) The girl suddenly jumped up from the backseat to play with her dad. She had the curliest brown hair I have ever seen, and she was all smiles. I could see her giggle as her daddy showered her with hugs and kisses. He talked to her and ran his fingers through her beautiful brown curls, fluffing her hair as he went. They were capturing a moment in time, before her older siblings arrived. It was just her and her daddy, enjoying small talk and loving one another.

I have thought about that glimpse in my rearview mirror for days. There was something so special about the two of them. It is a reminder of Jesus and how He loves His children. I'm not just talking about children in general, I am talking about all of His children, including you and me.

There are many stories I could tie into the rearview mirror picture, but my mind keeps returning to the Samaritan Woman. We looked at part of this story just a few pages back in the devotional, "The Poof." The Samaritan Woman slowly began to understand that Jesus was the Messiah. The One the Samaritans were watching for, but why did she finally believe He was the actual Messiah? She spent quality time with Jesus!

Remember Jewish people didn't talk to the Samaritans. They would often go around Samaria to avoid interacting with them at all. So, when Jesus said, *"Please give me a drink." (John*

4:7) this intrigued her. She immediately began asking Jesus questions and a conversation ensued. She wanted to know more about this Jewish man who was compassionate enough to speak to her, a Samaritan, who they typically despised.

Jesus answered each of her questions with a comment eluding to the fact that He was the Messiah. He never gave up and walked away from her. He didn't get frustrated with all of her questions, and begin to argue. He had a loving conversation with her, and with each reply to her questions, He revealed a little more about himself.

Jesus was loving on her just like the daddy in my rearview mirror was loving on his daughter. He was capturing that moment in time, with that one person—the Samaritan Woman.

How often do we spend quality time with the Messiah? We live in such a busy world that we often push away the One who loves us the most. The more time we spend with Jesus, the more we will get to know and understand Him. He longs to spend quality time with you, the person He is absolutely crazy about. God never grows tired of your questions or your rambling when you come to Him in prayer. He treasures that one-on-One quality time with the child He loves—YOU.

Find a quiet place and spend some quality time with Jesus today. Take a break from your busy life, and read *John 4:1-42*. As God reveals more of himself to you, remember *"But those who drink the water I give will never be thirsty again. It becomes a fresh, bubbling spring within them, giving them eternal life." (John 4:14).*

The Blood

I have been a blood donor most of my life, and I donated a few hours ago. It doesn't bother me to give blood, so I try to give as often as possible. It only takes an hour or two out of my day, and sometimes it leaves me a little tired the rest of the day. Today I was even a guinea pig for training purposes which didn't go well, so I have a bandage around both arms. But hey—she had to learn somehow and every donation helps save lives.

I thanked each of the workers as I was being processed through the center today. They are just as important to the process as the blood donors. I am able to donate, but I couldn't be a phlebotomist. I don't like to inflict pain on someone else!

Several years ago, my sister Linda was fighting a rare blood disease, aplastic anemia. As a result of blood donations, I was given six more months with my sister. She fought the good fight and had countless blood transfusions. I am so grateful for those months with my sister, and I pray my donations have a similar impact on the recipients.

The blood we donate saves lives, but the blood Jesus shed on the cross saves souls. However, it is up to us to spread the Good News with others. I expressed my gratitude today, but I didn't share a salvation message with anyone. I mentioned that I am a Christian author and speaker, but that is as far as the conversation went. I wish I was bolder about my faith in unknown surroundings, another hurdle I need to overcome. At the very least, I pray my willingness to be a guinea pig and my gratitude for their work left a good example of Christianity.

When I miss an opportunity to witness, I tend to be hard on myself. Then I remember God's wonderful grace, and confess my shortcomings. God is quick to forgive and brings me back into His presence.

I was going to use the following Bible verses in a previous devotional, but changed my mind. So, they have been in the *Bloom in God's Promises* document for months. On several occasions, I began to delete them, but always felt the nudge to leave them. So, I would hit the enter key several times to move them to the bottom of the document.

Today when I began to write, there they were. I reread them…again…and the first verse jumped off the page at me. God knew the day was coming when I needed this passage, not for this book, but for myself. What a wonderful reminder that when you and I miss the mark, and we will, He is there to rescue us. Even more powerful is the reminder that one day we will live in His presence in heaven without all of our flaws and mistakes.

> ***Now all glory to God, who is able to keep you from falling away and will bring you with great joy into his glorious presence without a single fault.*** *All glory to him who alone is God, our Savior through Jesus Christ our Lord. All glory, majesty, power, and authority are his before all time, and in the present, and beyond all time! Amen. (Jude 1:24-25 Emphasis added)*

Praise God for His wonderful grace, which rescues us time after time. I pray that you and I both become stronger and bolder in our faith. Remember, there is no greater donation, and no greater sacrifice than the blood Jesus shed on the cross for the forgiveness of our sins.

Dreary Autumn Day

It has been raining for hours, making for a dreary autumn day. The trees which were vibrant with fall colors are almost bare as the leaves fall into a pile below.

I should be thankful for the rain, but in late October the heavy rain is delaying harvest. On the flip side, Jim is running errands, so the house is quiet. The pitter-patter of the rain on the metal roof is soothing, and the quietness gives me time to gather my thoughts before I write. So even though it is depressing outside, I will enjoy the day.

Did you know? *"When the king smiles, there is life; his* ***favor*** *refreshes like a spring rain." (Proverbs 16:15 Emphasis added).* Paul also speaks of God's favor in his letter to the church of Philippi. He was in a Roman prison when he wrote the letter, so you could say it was raining in Paul's world too. Rather than feeling sorry for himself, he wrote a letter of thanks and encouragement to the church in Philippi.

I am blessed because my profession gives me quiet time with God as I search the Bible for great nuggets of truth and wisdom. However, my true joy comes when I share my thoughts with each of you.

My thoughts today are full of appreciation for you, and how God's favor is upon all of us. *"God knows how much I love you and long for you with the tender compassion of Christ Jesus." (Philippians 1:8).* Without your positive feedback, support, and encouragement, I would feel as if I was in prison with Paul on this rainy day.

God's Word also says, *"There will be glory and honor and peace from God for all who do good...For God does not show favoritism." (Romans 2:10-11).* Just because I am a Christian author, I have no greater connection to Jesus, and no added blessings from Him. God has no favorites. We are walking this Christian road together. Hand in hand. Heart to heart.

I am reminded of my key ministry verse, *"When we get together, I want to encourage you in your faith, but I also want to be encouraged by yours. (Romans1:12).* When we encourage one another, it lifts my spirits. So, thank you for all your continual encouragement. My heart truly overflows with gratitude for each of you. *"So it is right that I should feel as I do about all of you, for you have a special place in my heart.* ***You share with me the special favor of God.*** *" (Philippians 1:7a Emphasis added).*

Is it raining in your world? Your rain may be a physical pain or a mental anguish. Some have even experienced prison like Paul. If you battle depression, the rainy days can often add to your symptoms. The glorious news is that no matter your circumstances, God's favor is upon each of us, as we encourage one another to do His work.

"I pray that your love will overflow more and more, and that you will keep on growing in knowledge and understanding. May you always be filled with the fruit of your salvation." (Philippians 1:9, 11a).

Like the autumn leaves on a tree, allow your vibrant colors to shine as you do God's work, and remember His favor is upon you, even on a dreary autumn day.

Respect

I was entering a store when I noticed an elderly man with a cane walking slowly toward the door. As I waited patiently holding the door for him, he said, "I don't move very fast anymore."

I was about to reply when an older teenager rudely entered and walked around the man. There wasn't much space for him to pass the gentleman, and I was so afraid he would trip the man as he stormed in. As if that wasn't rude enough, he loudly said to his mother, "He's just an old man moving slow."

I stood there in shock! How could he treat this poor man with such disrespect? His actions and words were horrible! My first thought was to reach out and smack him, but I knew that wasn't the solution. His mother was embarrassed and didn't know what to say or do. She lowered her head, shrugged her shoulders and walked by as the older man shuffled along.

Where did we lose respect for others in this world? God's Word says, *"Stand up in the presence of the elderly, and show respect for the aged. (Leviticus 19:32)*. This verse is part of the Levitical rules, but Jesus summarized these rules by stating the two greatest commandments.

> *Jesus replied, "You must love the Lord your God with all your heart, all your soul, and all your mind. This is the first and greatest commandment. A second is equally important: Love your neighbor as yourself"*
> *(Matthew 22:37-39)*

Sadly, this teenager had not been taught the importance of respect and loving your neighbor. As an outsider looking in, his home life was probably lacking in discipline and love. As much as I wanted to correct him, I knew his problems were much deeper.

In this situation, it is much easier to love the elderly man than it was to love the teen. But the truth is we are called to love everyone. Jesus said, *"But to you who are willing to listen, I say, love your enemies! Do good to those who hate you. Bless those who curse you. Pray for those who hurt you. If you love only those who love you, why should you get credit for that? Even sinners love those who love them!" (Luke 6:27, 28, 32).*

It can be a challenge to love the unlovable of this world, but without our love will they ever know Jesus?

I was two hours from home when this incident happened. I will never cross paths with either of them again, but I can pray for them out of love. I pray the elderly man is able to provide for himself, or seek the assistance he needs. As for the teenager, I pray God gives him compassion for the elderly so he shows respect for them in the future. I pray both of these people find the physical and emotional healing they need in the future.

Points to Ponder

- What person in your life is "unlovable"?
- How can you show them respect by loving them, regardless of their flaws?
- Do your words and actions always show respect for others?

The House

It was in the fall of 2007 when we first looked at the house we now live. It is a beautiful home on 39 acres We didn't have to move, but noticed that this property was for sale just a few miles down the road. It had been on and off the market for years, at a very high price, but now it was a buyer's market. Unfortunately, the original owner and builder had passed away, and it was back on the market to settle his estate.

We of course went through the usual procedures. We made an offer. They counter offered. We raised our offer a little, and they countered again. Then the lawyer for the estate got involved. We met with him, but neither side would budge on the price, and the deal went dead. We knew no one was living here, so on numerous occasions throughout this process and even after meeting with the lawyer, we came here and prayed. We knew our offer was as high as we could afford, so we left it in God's hands.

Thanksgiving came and went and we both decided that we would not be moving. Then about ten days before Christmas Jim received a phone call asking if our offer to purchase the property was still available. Jim didn't tell me they called, instead he started all the necessary paperwork and put together a plan to surprise me on Christmas morning. To this day, he still tells everyone that he gave me a house for Christmas.

We know this property is a gift from God. Since all negotiating had ended, it was the power of prayer which reopened the door to purchase it. The house has it quirks and we have made a few changes, but I am blessed to live here. It is back a long lane where we are surrounded by our crops every year.

I share this story with you, not to brag, but as a testimony of how God has worked in our lives. We need to share our God stories with others, because that is what glorifies Him. Those firsthand examples of faith and answers to prayer, give the glory back to Him. When we share our testimonies, we have an impact on others.

The Samaritan Woman had an encounter with Jesus at the well and asked Him many questions. With each answer, Jesus reveals more and more about Himself, finally He says, *"I am the Messiah!" (John 4:26).*

The Samaritan Woman could have kept this knowledge to herself, but she didn't. She immediately ran to the town and shared her testimony with others. I love what happened next, *"The people came streaming from the village to see him." (John 4:30).*

Her firsthand testimony brought others to meet Jesus! If we keep quiet about God's miracles in our lives, how will others know what God is capable of doing?

The Samaritan Woman didn't nonchalantly say, "Oh by the way that guy up there claims to be the Messiah." There was excitement in her voice when she reached the village that day. *"Come and see a man who told me everything I ever did! Could he possibly be the Messiah?" (John 4:29).* Is there excitement in your voice when you speak about Jesus to others?

God gave Jim and I a house, a story we have shared multiple times. I don't know why I have not shared this story in my books before. What I do know is that it is God's timing, and today He nudged me to share my firsthand testimony.

I have always said, "I was after the house, and Jim was after the thirty-nine acres of farm ground." In reality, God was after our testimony. So, what is your God story and who can you share it with today?

Development

The economy is on the upswing, and so are the number of housing developments in our area. You don't have to travel far to see a house under construction, or an entire neighborhood being built. I am not against developments and progress, but I hate to see the farm ground in our area slowly disappear.

The good news is that farming technology is also under improvement and our yields are much higher than they were ten years ago. Sometimes I wonder if there will be enough land to grow food for all the animals and people, but it all seems to be part of God's greater plan. He blesses us with greater yields and provides food for His people regardless of the situation.

There are also ways to develop your ministry in life. One way to build a stronger witness is through your giving. God will always bless you with more than you have when you give with a cheerful heart.

> *For God is the one who provides seed for the farmer and then bread to eat. In the same way, he will provide and increase your resources and then produce a great harvest of generosity in you. Yes, you will be enriched in every way so that you can always be generous. And when we take your gifts to those who need them, they will thank God. So two good things will result from this ministry of giving—the needs of the believers in Jerusalem will be met, and they will joyfully express their thanks to God.*
> *(2 Corinthians 9:10-12)*

"He will provide and increase your resources." Did you catch the phrase? It is so amazing. We cannot out give God. It doesn't matter what we give, or where we give, but it does matter

how we give. *"You must each decide in your heart how much to give. And don't give reluctantly or in response to pressure. 'For God loves a person who gives cheerfully.'" (2 Corinthians 9:7).*

We need to develop a relationship with God and listen to discernment before we donate. Instead of giving to just anyone, we need to pray about our decision. Read God's Word and have a peace in our hearts about those in need.

About a year ago, I became acquainted with Mary Kate who was leaving for Montenegro to be a missionary. From the moment we met, I felt God tug on my heart to help her financially, and I have never regretted my decision.

She is doing God's work in Montenegro, and I am doing God's work here through my financial support. I do not miss the money, and in return I am blessed when I read her monthly newsletters about the lives she is impacting for Jesus. Though we give in different ways, we are both giving with a cheerful heart. Our work together is making a difference in the lives of others.

God is in the developing business. Houses are being built to provide shelter for His growing population. God helps us develop technology to improve crop production. He is developing a missionary team in Montenegro as more people are led to Christ. Best of all, God develops a passion within us to give cheerfully to those in need.

Anticipation

Since COVID19 hit this past spring, more of our supplies, merchandise, and presents are ordered online. Like a child awaiting Christmas, once the order has been placed, we anticipate its arrival.

How many days until it arrives? Will it meet my needs? Will it fit? Will it arrive on time? Will I like the color? There are so many questions as we patiently anticipate the delivery.

God designed us to be curious, it is part of our personalities. Just as we anticipate the arrival of a package, we often anticipate what heaven will be like. We aren't sure what to expect. How do we know what happens after death? Are we sure we will go to heaven?

My mother-in-law, Leah, was very confident that she would one day be in heaven. Per her request, she had a fork in her hand in her casket. Often at big family meals or at potluck dinners, someone will say, "Keep your fork!"

This common phrase is eluding to the dessert which is coming—the best part of the meal. Leah truly believed that the best part of her life was yet to come in heaven. Her desire was to be a witness of her faith in Jesus even after her death, by holding a fork in her hand. She wasn't scared of death, instead she anticipated her arrival on the streets of gold where she would praise Jesus for eternity.

Are you prepared for eternity? Have you received your package from God—the free gift of salvation?

> *For it is by grace you have been saved, through faith—and this is not from yourselves, it is the gift of God—not by works, so that no one can boast. (Ephesians 2:8-9 NIV)*

"It is the gift of God." It is hard to believe that God gives you this wonderful gift for free, but He does. We are accustomed to our earthly gifts. They may last for a season, or for a few years, but they will never last for eternity. This wonderful gift of grace is the most important package you will ever receive.

Heaven will be a beautiful place with streets of gold. We will all by singing and praising God for eternity. This is a place you don't want to miss!

On the flip side, Jesus gives us a brief picture of hell in *Matthew 13:49b-50 (NIV). "The angels will come and separate the wicked from the righteous and throw them into the blazing furnace, where there will be weeping and gnashing of teeth."*

I can't imagine living in agony for eternity, when we can live with Jesus. Can you? If you have not accepted your free gift of salvation, or if you question your salvation, please pray the sinner's prayer below.

We do not know what the future holds here on earth, but by accepting our free gift of grace, we can anticipate that the best is yet to come!

Dear Lord,
I know I am a sinner who is unworthy of Your love and grace. I understand this is a free gift from You. A package which contains my ticket into heaven. Please forgive me of my many sins. Wipe my slate clean, so I might live in your presence forever more. I anticipate my future in heaven where I will sing praises of joy to you for eternity. O thank you dear Jesus that the best is yet to come. I will be holding my fork in anticipation of my arrival one day! Amen and amen!

Dr. Livingstone

"There is one safe and happy place, and that is in the will of God.[vi]*"* ~ *Dr. David Livingstone*

David Livingstone was a medical missionary and explorer in Africa during the mid 19th century. Before he set sail for Africa, he completed his training as a doctor and missionary in Scotland and England. After several years, he traveled back to England, but his heart remained in Africa. A couple of years later, he returned to Africa to explore more, and to be a missionary to the African people.

In 1871, Henry Stanley was sent from England to locate Livingstone. He was successful, but Dr. Livingstone chose to stay in Africa to continue God's work. He died about a year later at the age of 60 from malaria and dysentery.

I cannot imagine the conditions of his explorations and missionary work in the mid 1800s. Life would have obviously been much easier for him in England or Scotland, where modernization was beginning to take place. Yet he chose to remain in God's will for his entire life. A life which was truly devoted to God, no matter the cost.

How many of us truly sacrifice our lives to the level of Dr. Livingstone? We are willing to follow God's will, but only if it fits into our plans, or only until the search party shows up to rescue us.

"Many are the plans in a person's heart, but it is the Lord's purpose that prevails." (Proverbs 19:21 NIV). I believe the Lord's purpose prevails with or without us. You can either align yourself with God's plan for your life, or allow Him to circumvent you and send someone else. Mordecai eluded to this very fact

when he asked Esther to approach King Xerxes to save the Jewish people.

> *"If you keep quiet at a time like this, deliverance and relief for the Jews will arise from some other place, but you and your relatives will die." (Esther 4:14a)*

Mordecai didn't beat around the bush, he was very blunt with Esther. You have a choice to make. You can either risk your life for the Jewish people, or God will find someone else who will.

I wonder how many opportunities we miss because we are unwilling to take a chance, or unwilling to serve in less the stellar circumstances. Sometimes our desire and God's will don't align, but when we allow God to change our heart, His purpose prevails. Then and only then, will our unwillingness be turned into pure joy.

> *Mordecai recorded these events and sent letters to the Jews near and far, throughout all the provinces of King Xerxes, calling on them to celebrate an annual festival on these two days. He told them to celebrate these days with feasting and gladness and by giving gifts of food to each other and presents to the poor. This would commemorate a time when the Jews gained relief from their enemies, when their sorrow was turned into gladness and their mourning into joy. (Esther 9:20-22)*

Suggested Readings

- Book of Esther
- Read more about the interesting explorations and missionary work of Dr. David Livingstone.

A Lucy

My friend Kim is known for the crazy things she does in life. Her husband, Tom, refers to these embarrassing moments as Lucy's. Which means, an incident like you would see on the *I Love Lucy* show. I had not seen Kim for quite some time and was excited to see her at Bible study. The first words out of my mouth were, "I pulled a Lucy last week," as I proceeded to tell her the following story.

I was on my way to the funeral home when I noticed the vehicle in front of me. At a quick glance, I was positive it was my sister Janet. The closer we got to the destination, the more convinced I was, because we weaved through town together. Both of us even turned onto the side street to park beside the funeral home. I pulled in directly behind her, and since we were a little early, I hopped out of my car to go sit in her backseat. With my hand on the door handle, the lady rolled down her window and said, "Can I help you?"

In a shocked voice I replied, "You're not my sister!"

I explained why I was about to crawl into her backseat, and we had a good chuckle. We had a short conversation about the parking meters and went our separate ways. Even though it was an embarrassing moment, I have done much worse.

All of this could have been avoided, if I had simply taken the time to focus on the car, and observe the situation better.

Clue #1: The lady had gray hair, Janet does not. Clue #2: Though it was the right type of vehicle it was the wrong color. This car was red, Janet's car is silver. (However, I'm not totally crazy because Janet's previous car was red. It just took me a while to remember that fact.)

In my situation, the result was simply a Lucy, but often haste causes us to struggle in life. We become enthusiastic and make quick decisions without considering the consequences of our actions.

Many people jump in and out of relationships or marriages without truly getting to know the person better before the relationship escalates. Others struggle with finding the right occupation. They move from job to job without taking the time to know what they desire. In both situations, they often forget to seek God's wisdom and direction.

A few extra moments of observation would have revealed that it was not my sister. Likewise, a few extra moments with Jesus, will help us discern the next step in our lives. We will never know all the future holds, but taking time to observe the situation, ask the right questions, and seek God's wisdom, can save us a great deal of undue heartache.

Don't allow the fear of the unknown to squelch your enthusiasm for life. If you do make a hasty decision, I pray it is a Lucy, because laughter is truly good for the soul.

> *Enthusiasm without knowledge is no good; haste makes mistakes. (Proverbs 19:2)*

> *He will once again fill your mouth with laughter and your lips with shouts of joy. (Job 8:21)*

KOKO

My friend signs her notes KOKO, which means "keep on keeping on." In other words, when life is difficult stay the course. Don't give up. Go the extra mile and keep being a witness for Christ.

In some respects KOKO is easier on paper than it is in person. There are times when we get weary and struggle in our faith. In those moments of frustration or discouragement, we need to dig deep within ourselves for the motivation to continue. Walking the Christian road alone is not sufficient in itself. We need to lean on one another, and tap into our faith in Jesus for strength.

The early Christians had incredible faith and endurance. They are true examples of KOKO. If they had given up, would the Christian church exist today?

Paul and Silas were among those who suffered for Christ. They were on their way to the house of prayer when a young slave girl repeatedly mocked them. After several days of her continual chanting, Paul demanded the evil spirit leave her, in the name of Jesus. The owners of the slave girl were furious because they earned a great deal of money from their fortune telling slave. They immediately demanded that Paul and Silas be thrown into prison.

> *A mob quickly formed against Paul and Silas, and the city officials ordered them stripped and beaten with wooden rods. They were severely beaten, and then they were thrown into prison. The jailer was ordered to make sure they didn't escape. So the jailer put them into the inner dungeon and clamped their feet in the stocks.*
> *(Acts 16:22-24)*

Their imprisonment was much different than prison today. They were stripped of their clothing, which also stripped them of their dignity. They were severely beaten. As if their pain and agony wasn't enough to keep them in prison, they were shackled deep within the prison. A place where only the worst prisoners were kept.

Just one of those abuses is enough to shake a person's KOKO attitude, but not Paul and Silas. Rather than giving up they praised Jesus! *"Around midnight Paul and Silas were praying and singing hymns to God, and the other prisoners were listening." (Acts 16:25).*

They possessed such a deep faith that they were able to praise God in their horrible prison conditions. I wonder, do you and I have that much faith today? The prison guard and his family came to know Jesus as their Savior that evening. All because Paul and Silas had a "keep on keeping on" attitude. He also had compassion for Paul and Silas and he nursed their wounds and took them to his home.

In order for Paul and Silas to dig deep within themselves to endure imprisonment, they praised the Lord. As God always does, He took their horrible circumstances and turned it into a great witness for Jesus. What a testimony of God's power and love!

Never give up. Never allow yourself to be beaten down. When difficulties arise, dig deep within and allow the Holy Spirit to lift you above your circumstances. When you "keep on keeping on," God will always meet you where you are. Over and over again, He will turn your situation into a God moment and a testimony of His greatness!

So...KOKO my dear friend!

The Spices

When the spices came tumbling off the shelf again today, I knew it was time to clean the spice cupboard. It is amazing what I found! I was expecting some duplicates, but I actually found three jars of basil. All of them were open and two had very little remaining. I found two jars of cinnamon sticks which I rarely use, so I put the sticks into the potpourri for a little extra fragrance. A few other bottles were combined, and voila it all fit in the cupboard, arranged by categories of course. (Yes my OCD side.)

Our lives are much like a spice cupboard. We allow extra problems to pile up causing an overflow of discontent on the shelves of our lives. Sometimes those troubles tumble off in all sorts of emotions. When this happens, or preferably before it happens, we need to take an inventory of the overflowing shelves in our lives. We need to discern which items are truly causing the overflow of discontent. It is often a small change which improves our attitude—like adjusting our priorities.

When we have too much work, and not enough Jesus, our attitudes get edgy. James warns us about the fine line between worldly pleasure and remaining close to God. Our first priority each day should be to draw close to Him.

> *So humble yourselves before God. Resist the devil, and he will flee from you. Come close to God, and God will come close to you. (James 4:7-8a)*

There is no greater fix for your attitude than giving your worries and concerns to Jesus. It is like the cinnamon sticks. You don't need the problems so put them in the potpourri, and allow Jesus to turn them into a sweet fragrance. He will definitely lighten your load.

Are you carrying around too many jars of basil? In other words, are you juggling too many projects at home or work? Ask Jesus for discernment on how to lighten your load. Often times we are overwhelmed by the big picture, but when it is divided into small pieces life looks much better. Just remember to keep Jesus as your first priority.

Putting Jesus first means living your life for Him. Every decision, every project, every step you take, should be centered around God's will. When you do this, it takes the stress off of you, and puts your life in God's hands. Rather than saying, "This is my plan for the next year," change your thought pattern to, *"If the Lord wants us to, we will live and do this or that." (James 4:15).*

There is never a greater time to rearrange the shelves of your life than today. Don't wait for that explosion of emotions to realize you are distant from the Lord. Draw close to Him today and enjoy the peace He will give you in every circumstance.

> *But the wisdom from above is first of all pure. It is also peace loving, gentle at all times, and willing to yield to others. It is full of mercy and the fruit of good deeds. It shows no favoritism and is always sincere. (James 3:17)*

Chicken Manure

I came home to a smell I dread—chicken manure. Our farm purchases the manure from a local chicken farm as fertilizer. The pile of manure has been here for a couple of days, and though it smelled a little, it is nothing like today. Oh, the horrible stench on the day it is spread on the field.

Slowly the smell goes away. A little rain helps and once the manure is worked into the ground, the odor completely disappears. But for today, the windows and doors are closed tight and I don't plan to exit again until necessary.

Our lives can also have an odor to them. Our sins pile up, and they begin to smell. When they are in a pile, we also tend to ignore them. A little sin here and another one there—none of them smell really bad. They are tolerable, or so we think. Then we realize how deep the pile is and we begin to spread them out before the Lord. As our pile of sins unfolds, we realize the horrible stench of each one.

Spreading them before the Lord is good though! We see our nasty sins, but God sees them as fertilizer. He uses every sin in our broken lives for His good. Each sin has its own stench, which serves a reminder of where we were. Followed by a sweet aroma of where who are with Christ. It is amazing how God can turn the horrible stench of sin into something beautiful!

If anyone's sins had a stench, it was Saul (Paul). *"Saul was one of the witnesses, and he agreed completely with the killing of Stephen." (Acts 8:1).* Stephen was the first martyr to give up his life for the gospel of Christ. He was known for his strong faith, his leadership, and teaching abilities. However, Saul was doing everything possible to stop the early church, and to him Stephen's death was a victory. What a horrible sin to put into the pile. Saul literally allowed and agreed with the death of Stephen.

Following Stephen's death, Saul requested permission to travel to Damascus to persecute more believers. He believed it was the next step necessary to stop the Christian movement. He planned to bring the Christians, both men and women, back to Jerusalem in chains.

But on the road to Damascus, Saul had an encounter with Jesus. All of his sins with their horrible stench were suddenly revealed. *"Saul! Saul! Why are you persecuting me?" (Acts 9:4b).*

Saul instantly knew he was wrong to persecute the church and to agree with Stephen's death. All of the sinful stench in Saul's life was suddenly spread before the Lord. The moment Saul was converted and baptized in Christ, that horrible smell of sin became fertilizer for his growth as a missionary. Saul went on to serve Christ in mighty ways, and he too suffered for the gospel of Christ for years.

When Saul had his encounter with Jesus that day, did Stephen's dying words echo in his mind?

> *"As they stoned him, Stephen prayed, "Lord Jesus, receive my spirit." He fell to his knees, shouting, "Lord, don't charge them with this sin!" And with that he died." (Acts 7:59-60)*

Our sins can have a great stench when spread before the Lord, but if our heart is true to Jesus, our stench becomes fertilizer to lead others to Christ. Are you sharing your conversion story? Like Stephen and Saul, allow your testimony to be a witness of God's grace. Share with others how God changed your life which had a stench similar to chicken manure, into a life of grace devoted to Jesus!

Stuck in Neutral

It recently came to my attention that I was stuck in neutral about my life. My home and its view across the field, my surroundings, and even my relationship with Jesus were all just existing. I had developed a stuck in the middle-of-the-road attitude.

A neighbor stopped by to drop off some paperwork. Even though we have been friends for years, she had not been to our home. She remarked about the beautiful woodwork, the spacious family room, and our great location back off of the road. Before she left, she commented about the beautiful view from our deck, at least three times. I responded, "We see a lot of deer out here once the crops are off," but my heart was saying, "Yeah it's okay." Even after all of her admiration, I didn't see the splendor of it all.

As I was sitting down for breakfast the following morning, Jim and I spotted three deer pretty close to our house. I realized it was a message from God about my stuck-in-neutral life. If I am anywhere else on vacation, I would be excited to see wildlife. In my own back yard, I had no appreciation for all He has given us.

Everything which surrounds me is a gift from God which I have taken for granted. The house with its beautiful woodwork. The location back off the road. The view where I often see deer in my backyard. Most of all, the human desire to fellowship with the Lord.

It is easy for us to become so used to our surroundings that we don't appreciate them. We see them every day and instead of viewing them with a grateful heart, we become disenchanted, always believing there is something better. Like the old adage says, "The grass is greener on the other side of the fence."

The same is true about our walk with Jesus. We can become so middle-of-the-road, that we forget our relationship should be dynamic. Jesus doesn't expect us to stay status quo, He expects us to grow, and draw closer to Him.

When the Psalmist wrote Psalm 42, it is obvious he longed to restore his relationship with the Lord. Within him was a thirst for fellowship with God, one that we too need to feel.

As the deer pants for streams of water,
so my soul pants for you, my God.
My soul thirsts for God, for the living God.
When can I go and meet with God?
(Psalm 42:1-2 NIV)

God needs to be the leap in our step and the joy in our hearts. God and only God can restore our stuck-in-neutral attitude and bring us back to a place of pure joy. A time where we truly appreciate our surroundings, our family, our hard work, and our God.

Are you stuck in neutral? I recommend you open your Bible to the book of Psalms and begin to read. It doesn't matter which one, just allow Him to speak to your heart and renew your spirit. He will help you kick your life out of neutral. And when He does, *"He makes you as surefooted as a deer, enabling you to stand on mountain heights." (Psalm 18:33).*

Hymn of Promise

We sang a hymn at church Sunday which Jim and I had never heard before. "Hymn of Promise" written by Natalie Sleeth in 1985. Since we didn't know the melody, we really couldn't sing along, but we both loved the words. If you don't know the song, I recommend you read the lyrics or listen to the song. It talks about the many promises of God.

The first stanza talks about how there is a flower within every bulb, and a butterfly will emerge from every cocoon. As I read and reread the lyrics, all I can think of is Bloom with Jesus! The next two stanzas talk about our hope in Jesus and spending an eternity with Him. What wonderful promises.

Not every devotion within this book contains the word promise, but the underlying theme is always that God is our hope and strength no matter our trials or our joys. The tagline for this book, *Daily Devotions to Walk a Consistent and Confident Pathway with Jesus* are words to encourage you. Life is difficult, but with Jesus life is wonderful. In order for us to a walk with Jesus consistently, and confidently on a daily basis, we need to lean on God's promises.

I went to www.biblegateway.com and typed the word **promise**. Look at this list showing the number of times promise is found in the Bible.

364 - New International Version (NIV)

128 - New Living Translation (NLT)

128 - New King James Version (NKJV)

279 - The Message (MSG)

You get the picture. Not all of these references contain the word promise, but they are still a reflection of God's promise to always love His people. No matter which version of the Bible you prefer, you are going to find promise after promise written to us.

God's promises were real years ago, and they are still true today. The promise spoken to Abram in *Genesis 15:1* is timeless and applies to our current lives. *"Some time later, the Lord spoke to Abram in a vision and said to him, 'Do not be afraid, Abram, for I will protect you, and your reward will be great.'"* Your name may not be Abram, but God will still protect you.

And the last reference found in all three versions is the greatest promise of all! *"And this is what he promised us—eternal life." (1 John 2:25 NIV).*

From God's protection to eternal life with the Father! It just doesn't get any better! Those are just two of the promises our amazing God has given us.

We are so much more than a bulb containing a flower. We are God's masterpiece, which was created in His image. When we believe in the promises woven throughout scripture, we walk a consistent and confident pathway with Jesus.

So, what are you waiting for? Bloom with Jesus! Bloom like a flower, especially one cultivated for its beauty, and become an irrepressible disciple!

For encouragement, more devotionals and inspiration, follow my blog, *Bloom with Jesus*, at https://maryrodman.com/blog

Curiosity

I had forgotten how curious cows can be until I drove by a pasture field the other day. The electric company was setting new poles along the road, and they had some of their equipment in the pasture. The cows were walking around the equipment investigating. They approached slowly and put their heads down close to the equipment and poles. They didn't appear to be upset, they were just curious. Something was definitely different in their familiar surroundings and they were trying to figure it out.

We too are curious people. We want to know when God is going to do this or that. How much longer do we need to wait? How will it happen? Even the disciples were curious and asked Jesus questions throughout His ministry.

Just before Jesus ascended to heaven they asked, *"'Lord, are you at this time going to restore the kingdom to Israel?' He said to them, 'It is not for you to know the times or dates the Father has set by his own authority. But you will receive power when the Holy Spirit comes on you; and you will be my witnesses in Jerusalem, and in all Judea and Samaria, and to the ends of the earth.'" (Acts 1:7b-8 NIV).*

After Jesus said these words, He ascended to heaven, and two angels appeared among them. *"Men of Galilee," they said, "why do you stand here looking into the sky? This same Jesus, who has been taken from you into heaven, will come back in the same way you have seen him go into heaven." (Acts 1:11 NIV).*

Immediately the disciples left the Mount of Olives and returned to Jerusalem. They didn't seem to question the who, what, when, where and why of the situation. They had witnessed Jesus ascension with their own eyes, and believed everything He said. As the disciples waited, they did everything they could, based on the instructions Jesus left them.

They stepped out in faith and immediately began the necessary preparations. They formed the first church meeting, and selected Matthias as the apostle to replace Judas Iscariot. Rather than worrying about what would happen next, they prayed for God's guidance and got organized.

All of this happened prior to the day of Pentecost, and even though the Holy Spirit had not arrived yet, Jesus had given the disciples three important messages.

Don't worry about when Jesus will return.

After I leave, the Holy Spirit will come.

You will become my witnesses and build the church.

We also need to follow the advice of Jesus. All too often we spend our time curious about the who, what, when, where and why, rather than following the Holy Spirit to do God's work. It is okay to be curious like a cow, but don't be obsessed with the details, take some kind of action and God will show up.

As it says in *1 Thessalonians 5:1-2 (NIV), "Now, brothers and sisters, about times and dates we do not need to write to you, for you know very well that the day of the Lord will come like a thief in the night."* Our job is to simply follow the nudging of the Holy Spirit and be a witness about the Good News.

Hydroplane

On our recent trip to Florida, Jim drove in and out of rain for two days. Just when we thought it was over, it found us again. He prefers to use the cruise control when driving, and it made me a little nervous that we might hydroplane. We arrived safe and sound last night and fortunately the rain had ceased for the unpacking.

Traveling on the wet and dry roads is like traveling through life. The dry roads are those smooth patches when everything is going great. No worries. No fears. No frustrations. You have the cruise control set and you are enjoying life to its fullest.

The next thing you know it is sprinkling, causing wet patches here and there on the pavement of your life. Even though little problems have cropped up, you are still joyful and cruising along.

Then the weather switches from sprinkles to solid rain. Maybe you are stressed at work with deadlines and sales goals. Your children are struggling with school issues. The baby is teething and you have many sleepless nights. You long for a vacation, but it is not in your budget.

Before you know it, it is storming! The rain is pouring and your life is about to hydroplane out of control. You long for some dry patches in the road, where you once felt joyful and safe.

The disciples experienced dry patches in the roadway of life too. They had days of sprinkles and even days of rain. But one day when they were sailing on the Sea of Galilee, a horrible storm blew in. As experienced sailors, they knew the risks involved with the storm and began to panic. They had witnessed Jesus performing many miracles and knew He was their only hope to be rescued. *"Jesus was sleeping. The disciples went and woke him up, shouting, 'Lord, save us! We're going to drown!'" (Matthew 8:24b-25).*

Before Jesus rebuked the winds, He chastised the disciples. *"Why are you afraid? You have so little faith!" (Matthew 8:26).* We are often like the disciples. We know God can handle the sprinkles and the rain in our lives, but panic during the storms. Why are we so afraid to give God the wheel when our lives are hydroplaning out of control?

If Jesus can calm the storms of nature, He can calm the storms of our lives. He will turn the rain-soaked roads back into dry patches of life where we were joyful and calm. Don't be like the disciples and question His capabilities. The closer you are to Jesus on the dry patches of road, the more faith you will have when the storms arrive.

The disciples knew Jesus could save them on the Sea of Galilee, and they were still amazed that He had the power to calm the seas. It simply was not the outcome they expected. They were looking for a miracle, but not a miracle where Jesus defied nature.

If God can rebuke the storms of nature, He most definitely can dry the road ahead of you in the midst of a storm. Remember to give Jesus full control of your life, before you hydroplane. Like the disciples, you will be amazed how Jesus will truly save you.

> *When the storms of life come, the wicked are whirled away, but the godly have a lasting foundation. (Proverbs 10:25)*

The Wedding Dress

My friend Angie is getting married and I had the pleasure of helping her select a wedding dress. When we arrived at the dress shop, a young lady greeted us and said she would be Angie's assistant to find the perfect dress.

She asked Angie a few questions and began to pull dresses from the rack. Of course, Angie tried on the ones she liked the best, and we were both disappointed. Not fancy enough. Not flattering to her figure. Not enough lace or too much lace. She finally put one on that was in the okay category, but it still wasn't what she was looking for.

After seeing this dress on Angie, our assistant disappeared to the back and came out with another dress. Neither Angie or myself would have picked this dress off the rack, but our assistant knew exactly what she was doing. It had some of the same features as the previous dress, yet it was styled differently. Angie went into the dressing room with a pessimistic attitude and emerged with a beaming smile. The dress was perfect and there was no need to look further.

Just moments prior, Angie was beginning to get a little discouraged. She didn't have to try on one more dress, but she persevered based on the advice of someone else. This lady had seen Angie in numerous dresses. She was also very trained and had an eye for fashion. After a couple of failures, she knew exactly which dress was going to be perfect.

Like our wedding dress assistant, there are times in our lives when we need the wisdom of someone more experienced. Godly mentors as essential to our Christian growth. There are many examples of mentors throughout the Bible as well.

Paul was a mentor to Timothy, a young believer in Lystra. Timothy made a commitment early in his life to serve the Lord, but he was young and timid. He continually looked to Paul for advice and encouragement. Even in times of failure, he persevered as Paul continually helped him grow as a Christian.

In his second letter to Timothy, Paul reminds him that he will face opposition for his beliefs, but not to be discouraged. In spite of this opposition in his life, Timothy needed to stand firm for what he knew to be true and right. What wonderful advice for us today too.

> *But you must remain faithful to the things you have been taught. You know they are true, for you know you can trust those who taught you. You have been taught the holy Scriptures from childhood, and they have given you the wisdom to receive the salvation that comes by trusting in Christ Jesus. (2 Timothy 3:14-15)*

I love the advice in the very first sentence! "*You must remain faithful to the things you have been taught.*" Don't be discouraged if you are a young Christian, or even if you are a seasoned Christian who is wavering in your faith. Lean on the wisdom of others to see you through. Just because a person is older than you, it doesn't mean they are a good Christian mentor either. Angie is 10 years younger than me, but she has been a faithful Christian friend and one of my mentors for over twenty years. A good mentor has strong faith, Biblical knowledge, and has persevered through trials themselves.

Life can be like trying on wedding dresses, sometimes you become discouraged and are ready to give up. Never give up on your faith, *remember the things you have been taught*! Seek wisdom from your mentors, and persevere. Overcoming the situation will prepare you for the perfect fit when your next big Christian decision comes in life.

Suggested Scripture

- *Acts 16:1-5*
- *2 Timothy 4:10-17*

Math Problem

My oldest granddaughter Mya is learning multiplication and division in school. She was working on homework and was stuck on the problem, 3 x 10 = 6 x __. She asked me for help, thinking I would give her the answer, but of course I didn't.

She prodded me by saying, "Grandma, I know three times ten equals thirty, but I don't know what times six equals thirty."

I stopped working to help, but encouraged her to work the problem herself. I started by asking, "What is six times one?"

"Six," she replied. I proceeded up the multiplication tables and she quickly replied with the correct answers until I asked, "What is six times five?

Silence. I had reached the root of the problem. She didn't have that answer memorized and she had to do the work to figure it out. She looked at me and smiled, but her brain was working the problem as she counted in her head. Finally she replied, "Thirty," and realized she had the answer for her homework.

All too often we don't do the necessary homework to grow in our Christian faith either. It is much easier to ask someone else for answers, rather than to doing research ourselves. Plus, it takes discipline and hard work to grow as a Christian.

The disciples didn't learn how to be the leaders of the first church overnight, or by sitting in the pew on Sunday morning. They studied under Jesus for three years. They asked questions of Jesus. Should we pay taxes? *(Mark 12:14).* They asked Jesus to explain the meaning to many parables. *(Matthew 13:10).* How do we pray? *(Luke 11:1).* With each question they asked Jesus, their faith grew stronger as they applied the lessons to their lives.

It is the same for you and me. The more questions we ask of Jesus in prayer, the more answers we will receive. We have at our fingertips the most amazing book of instructions, the Bible, and we often ignore it and look elsewhere for advice.

Like Mya, we need to apply ourselves to study and do our homework each day. Each time you read God's Word, you will find something new to apply to your life.

We are all workers for Jesus who need to do our homework each day. We need to pray like Jesus taught us to pray, and ask Him for wisdom.

> *Work hard so you can present yourself to God and receive his approval. Be a good worker, one who does not need to be ashamed and who correctly explains the word of truth. (2 Timothy 2:15)*

Remember how important your Christian growth is as you daily seek more knowledge. The deeper your knowledge, the stronger your faith. The stronger your faith, the closer you will be to Jesus.

My child, listen to what I say, and treasure my commands.
Tune your ears to wisdom, and concentrate on understanding.
Cry out for insight, and ask for understanding.
Search for them as you would for silver; seek them like hidden treasures.
Then you will understand what it means to fear the Lord, and you will gain knowledge of God.
For the Lord grants wisdom! From his mouth come knowledge and understanding.
He grants a treasure of common sense to the honest.
He is a shield to those who walk with integrity.
He guards the paths of the just and protects those who are faithful to him.
(Proverbs 2:1-8)

Mary Rodman

Tangled Yarn

I just spent the last hour sorting and untangling three tubs of yarn. I know what you're thinking, three tubs! Well, let me put in a disclaimer. A great deal of the yarn was given to me, and about a year ago a craft store near my home was going out of business, so I stocked up on certain colors. Now that I have justified my three tubs of yarn, I will continue with my story.

I crochet in the evenings, a hobby I picked up the past several years. I make a variety of items, but I prefer to make what I call Blooming Critters. They are one of a kind crochet animals. Each one seems to have its own personality, which makes them my favorite projects.

It takes a multitude of colors to make Blooming Critters. Pastel bunnies, yellow ducks, blue hippos, pink elephants and my latest was Buckeye the calico cat. Buckeye was mostly scarlet and gray, thus his name. (For my OSU fans—Go Bucks!). When you stir the tubs of yarn looking for colors, eventually all the loose ends become tangled. I try my best to put the same type of yarn back in the same tub, but there are also times when I just lift a lid and give it a toss. It was to the point where I couldn't find the necessary yarn, so it was time to sort.

Our lives are much like the tangled yarn. How many times have we simply opened the lid and given our problems a toss? Our nerves get frayed, and our insides become knots. Soon we are one big tangled mess, and we feel like we are in the wrong tub in life.

We are useless to our family and friends if we are tangled in knots. We can even become a burden to others. So how do we untie the knots? You could take a vacation, and dust your problems under the rug for a while, but typically when you return you instantly become a tangled mess again. The true "Un-tangler" is Jesus. True mercy and wisdom come from the Lord.

David was a man after God's own heart, and he wrote many Psalms where he pleaded with God for comfort. He often cried out to God and asked him to untangle his frayed ends, and give his life purpose and direction. We can relate to many of David's feelings, and I encourage you to find Psalms of comfort on your own. I find the words of *Psalm 142* to be very comforting. When our nerves are frayed and our insides are in knots, we feel no one else cares, but God always listens to our woes and He cares about our frayed ends.

I cry out to the Lord; I plead for the Lord's mercy.
I pour out my complaints before him and tell him all my troubles.
When I am overwhelmed, you alone know the way I should turn.
Wherever I go, my enemies have set traps for me.
I look for someone to come and help me, but no one gives me a passing thought!
No one will help me; no one cares a bit what happens to me.
Then I pray to you, O Lord. I say, "You are my place of refuge.
You are all I really want in life.
Hear my cry, for I am very low.
Rescue me from my persecutors, for they are too strong for me.
Bring me out of prison so I can thank you.
The godly will crowd around me, for you are good to me."
(Psalm 142:1-7)

Covid-19 Christmas

Can I just say I am tired of social distancing? I know it is a necessity, but having Christmas from the front door just isn't the same as hugging your grandchildren.

Our youngest grandson Lincoln is high risk. I refer to him as our miracle grandchild. First of all, he was born with the umbilical cord wrapped around his neck. The majority of the babies who have this die while still in the womb. Second, he was born with only one kidney and a kink in his urethra, which the doctors can hopefully fix when he is a little older. The kidney issue makes him very high risk for COVID because a high fever could damage his only kidney. In order to maintain his safety, Grandpa and I did a porch visit for Christmas.

The older two Jackson and Kennedy were standing at the door watching for us. They jumped up and down when we pulled in the driveway and their excitement melted my heart. We passed the presents in the door and sat on the porch to watch them open gifts. Jackson was excited to open a track hoe and as we left Kennedy was hugging the crochet unicorn I made her.

We had brought Lincoln, who is about one, a huge stuffed train. He laid his head down on the train to cuddle it. Then he discovered that each section of the train had a button. He pushed the first button and smiled. It didn't take him long to catch on, and he started pushing all the buttons.

I had also crocheted each of them a snowman. He picked up his snowman and pushed the button, but nothing happened. He tried several times and then brought it to Mommy for help. She told him that the snowman didn't make noise, and we all had a chuckle.

Watching Lincoln cuddle with his train reminded me of the importance of touch and the closeness to others which we are missing due to Covid-19. There is something special about a hug or the touch of a loved one holding your hand when you need comfort.

Often when Jesus healed someone it was through the power of His touch. The woman who suffered from bleeding for twelve years thought, *"If I can just touch his robe. I will be healed." (Matthew 9:21),* as she reached out to touch the hem of his robe.

Just moments later Jesus said, *'"The girl isn't dead; she's only asleep." Jesus went in and took the girl by the hand, and she stood up!' (Matthew 9:24b, 25b).*

After Jesus left the girl's home two blind men began to follow Him.

Jesus asked them, "Do you believe I can make you see?"

"Yes Lord," they told him, "we do."

Then he touched their eyes and said, "Because of your faith, it will happen." (Matthew 9:28b-29).

All of these miracles happened on the same day and each was centered around Jesus' touch. This is just a small example of the healing power of touch which Christ displays.

It was important for Jesus to physically touch others. The touch of His hand brought healing. Not always a physical healing, sometimes simply a calm emotional healing. It is important for us to experience the same healing power of touch. A little one is comforted by a hug when they are hurt. Children experience an adult's love through a hug, or simply the touch of your hands. Even as adults, there is comfort when a someone holds your hand, or touches your shoulder when you are in turmoil.

Being unable to touch my grandchildren saddens my heart. I know it is best to keep my distance, but I feel as if a bond has been broken or lost, due to the lack of touch. We will continue to make the best of the situation in 2021 and pray that we will soon be able to hold them in our arms again. I can't wait to give them a big Grandma bear hug.

Whether you read this devotion in the midst of Covid-19 or afterward, always remember the importance of touch. Follow Jesus example and show others how much we love them by the touch of your hand or a hug.

"He said to them, "Let the children come to me. Don't stop them!" Then he took the children in his arms and placed his hands on their heads and blessed them." (Mark 10:14b,16).

Lincoln (age 1) with his wonderful smile.

Gratitude

Whenever I have a fortune cookie, I have to read my fortune. Most of them are more of a puzzle than wisdom, but on occasion I receive one that makes me think.

This fortune has been sitting on my desk for a couple of weeks, and I read it periodically. "Gratitude is not only the greatest of virtues, but the parent of all others." I believe it is important to live a life of gratitude, but I would like to rephrase the fortune for you. "Gratitude **toward Jesus** is not only the greatest of virtues, but the parent of all others." After all, where would we be without a Savior!

When you realize that without Jesus you are nothing and have nothing, it puts a whole new twist on the fortune. Paul is very poignant about this fact in these words.

> *I thank Christ Jesus our Lord, who has given me strength to do his work. He considered me trustworthy and appointed me to serve him, even though I used to blaspheme the name of Christ. In my insolence, I persecuted his people. But God had mercy on me because I did it in ignorance and unbelief. Oh, how generous and gracious our Lord was! He filled me with the faith and love that come from Christ Jesus. (1 Timothy 1:12-14)*

Paul was trained as a Pharisee, which made him very knowledgeable of the scriptures. He felt the Christian movement was against Judaism, and fought fiercely against the Christians. Yes, Paul even persecuted them prior to his salvation. *(Acts 9:1-9).*

God took all of Paul's strengths—his knowledge of the scriptures, and weaknesses—persecuting Christians, and turned him into a great missionary. No other person in history has impacted Christianity like Paul. Our gratitude needs to go beyond Jesus. We need to also be thankful for Paul, because he brought the gospel to the Gentiles. Without his hard work and dedication to the Lord, we would not have the Christian foundation we have today.

Like Paul, we too are sinners. We all make mistakes, have faith struggles, and question our abilities to be a disciple of Christ. Yet we are all worthy to be a servant and a witness of Jesus Christ.

God used Paul in mighty ways, and for that I am truly thankful. Jesus Christ took all of my sins to the cross, an act of kindness I will never be able to repay. However, I choose to live a life of gratitude toward Jesus and to be His faithful disciple in the work He grants me. I will hold tight to the truths Paul wrote to the Gentiles, so many years ago. These Words are God breathed, timeless, and true for all who believe in the power of Jesus.

> *Every time I think of you, I give thanks to my God. Whenever I pray, I make my requests for all of you with joy, for you have been my partners in spreading the Good News about Christ from the time you first heard it until now. And I am certain that God, who began the good work within you, will continue his work until it is finally finished on the day when Christ Jesus returns. (Philippians 1:3-6)*

Points to Ponder

- What "good work" has Jesus begun within you which you need to finish?
- What is your greatest fear, or hurdle which keeps you from becoming a true disciple of Jesus?
- Find a scripture which erases that fear and helps you understand true grace.
- Record your daily gratitude each day for a month. You will be amazed at the changes in your heart.

Old MacDonald

Old MacDonald had a farm, E-I-E-I-O. And on that farm, he had Blooming Critters, E-I-E-I-O. With a hippo here, and unicorns there. Here a chick, there a cat everywhere bunnies go. Old MacDonald had a farm, E-I-E-I-O.

I am Old MacDonald and I have a bunch of Blooming Critters. My granddaughters and I attend 3-4 craft shows a year. They have their Kid's Corner with painted rocks and button pictures. I sell my Christian books, and one-of-a-kind crochet animals, which I call Blooming Critters.

My house has been a disaster with crafts strewn from one end to the other as the girls and I have accumulated items to sell. Unfortunately, the craft show was canceled due to the coronavirus. Regretfully, I put the Blooming Critters back into their corral (plastic tubs). Just like the ninety-nine sheep in the parable of the Lost Sheep. They are now safe and sound. And yes, there is one lost critter, an incomplete bunny which I will add later.

My disappointment has nothing to do with the crafts themselves. My greatest sorrow is that I might miss a chance to witness to the Lost Sheep. Selling my devotional books at craft shows gives me the opportunity to share my faith with others. The books easily open the door for conversations which otherwise may never occur. I know this situation is in God's hands and it is all in His timing. If the Lost Sheep planned to attend tomorrow, they will probably attend when the show is rescheduled.

The parable of the Lost Sheep is dear to my heart because it convicts me to witness to the lost. Each book in the *Bloom Daily Devotional Series* contains ninety-nine devotions. Why such an odd number? A reminder to pray for the Lost Sheep. So, while I wait for the next craft show, I will pray.

This parable can be found in the gospels of *Matthew* and *Luke*. Jesus shares this story to emphasize the importance of each person. As Christians, we are part of the ninety-nine sheep who are safe in the corral. Since we are protected, God will leave us and go search for the one who is lost. *"He [Jesus] does not want anyone to be destroyed, but wants everyone to repent." (2 Peter 3:9)*. Therefore, He constantly searches for the lost souls.

As Christians, our job is to share the gospel with those who are lost. Somewhere in your heart, you have a God story which can impact an unbeliever. When you pray for the Lost Sheep, also pray for the opportunity to share your faith. God will use you to reach the lost because: *"There is more joy in heaven over one lost sinner who repents and returns to God than over ninety-nine others who are righteous and haven't strayed away!" (Luke 15:7)*.

I finished my lost critter tonight and added the bunny to the corral. May you complete your job by sharing the gospel with a Lost Sheep who needs Jesus!

> *"If a man has a hundred sheep and one of them wanders away, what will he do? Won't he leave the ninety-nine others on the hills and go out to search for the one that is lost? And if he finds it, I tell you the truth, he will rejoice over it more than over the ninety-nine that didn't wander away! In the same way, it is not my heavenly Father's will that even one of these little ones should perish."*
> *(Matthew 18:12-14)*

Conclusion—The Promise

In his book *50 Days of Heaven* by Randy Alcorn, he shares a story of a professional singer who missed the wedding banquet. Below is this wonderful analogy rewritten in my own words.

> A professional singer was invited to sing for the wedding of a very rich man. She was honored to be the guest at the wedding and perform her beautiful music. She and her husband were anxious to attend the wedding reception, knowing it would be the greatest celebration they would ever attend.
>
> The party was to be held on the top floor of a well-known, high rise building, which overlooked the city. She knew the banquet would be immaculate, from the decorations to the meal itself, it would be a once in a lifetime experience.
>
> Her and her husband were among the guest who followed the bride and groom up a beautiful, winding, gold and glass staircase. The wedding couple cut a ribbon at the top of the staircase and invited their guests into the banquet hall.
>
> When the singer and her husband neared the entrance to the banquet hall, they were greeted by the maître d' who requested their names. She politely introduced herself, and he searched the guest book for their names, but he could not find them on the list. The maître d' requested that she spell her name, but their names were still not found on the list.
>
> She said, "There has to be some mistake. I am the wedding singer. I have to be on the list. Please look again."
>
> He replied, "I'm sorry but you are not on the list of guests. If you are not on the list, you cannot attend the banquet."

He motioned for a waiter to escort them to the service elevator. On their way to the elevator, they had a glimpse of the beautiful banquet. Ice sculptures, smoked salmon, cocktail shrimp, the finest of linens and beautiful decorations throughout the banquet hall. There was an orchestra dressed in white tuxedos, who would soon be playing their angelic-like music. The banquet hall was radiant, but they could not enter

The elevator door opened, and the waiter pushed "G" for the parking garage. They were sent away, with only a glimpse of what could have been. The couple drove for miles in silence, unable to speak about the horrible mix up which had occurred.

Her husband finally broke the silence and asked, "What happened? Why were we not on the list for the reception?"

With tears streaming down her face, she responded, "I was extremely busy when the invitation came and I didn't RSVP. At the time I thought, 'I am the wedding singer, so surely I am already on the list for the reception.'"

She was sad they had missed the immaculate wedding reception, but her heart truly ached when she realized they had just experienced a real-life parable. An example of those who will never attend Christ's wedding banquet one day, simply because they were too busy to RSVP.

Jesus is preparing the most immaculate banquet you could ever attend. Friends and loved ones will be celebrating and worshipping God. Angels will be singing. No more pain and suffering. Only praise and glory. Heaven will have streets of gold with angelic singing. We will be in Christ's presence forevermore.

Everyone is invited, but only those who RSVP will be able to attend the banquet. Don't allow the craziness of your life keep you from entering the greatest banquet of all time. Those who are escorted to the elevator won't be going to the parking garage. They will have missed their last opportunity to spend eternity with Christ.

This book is about God's promises. The greatest promise God has given us is the free gift of salvation. We don't deserve it, and we can't earn it. It is His free gift of grace when we proclaim Christ Jesus as our Lord and Savior. There is no other way to heaven except through Jesus.

> *Jesus told him, "I am the way, the truth, and the life. No one can come to the Father except through me. (John 14:6)*

> *When God our Savior revealed his kindness and love, he saved us, not because of the righteous things we had done, but because of his mercy. He washed away our sins, giving us a new birth and new life through the Holy Spirit. He generously poured out the Spirit upon us through Jesus Christ our Savior. Because of his grace he made us right in his sight and gave us confidence that we will inherit eternal life. (Titus 3:4-7)*

> *For God loved the world so much that he gave his one and only Son, so that everyone who believes in him will not perish but have eternal life. God sent his Son into the world not to judge the world, but to save the world through him. (John 3:16-17)*

I pray you know and understand this free gift of salvation. I look forward to meeting you at the wedding banquet in heaven with Jesus one day!

For those who have questions about salvation and the promise of living with Christ for eternity, I would love to connect with you and pray with you. To contact me and for further information go to:
https://maryrodman.com/pages/god-s-promises

Additional Inspiration

Please enjoy the following poem written by my friend and sister in Christ, Lori Zimmerman. Her words express the importance standing in the gap for a loved one by praying, and standing on the promises of God. My prayer is that you will always *Bloom in God's Promises*!

I Stood at the Window

I stood at the window and watched you this morning.
I watched as you walked to the barn, as you do each day and opened the door to begin your work.

I stood at the window and watched you this morning.
You walked to the edge of the wet field and looked. You were looking, but I know you were thinking.
I imagine you were thinking, "When God? When will you allow this field (and all the others) to be dry enough to plant seeds?"

I stood at the window and watched you this morning.
I know how hard it is to gaze at that water standing and not be able to do what you love—to plant.
In your heart you know God is in control, but I am sure you have to keep reminding yourself of that.

I stood at the window and watched you this morning.
I felt tears in my eyes as I thought about how helpless you must feel. I feel it too.
There is nothing you can do to dry the fields and there is nothing I can do to help you.

I stood at the window and watched you this morning.
I watched you walk back to the barn looking somewhat defeated.
But I see you find work to do. You will not be idle.

I stood at the window and watched you this morning.

I watched you talk to the young man who has come to help.
I imagine you talking about how much it rained last night and the plan for the day.
But, I also imagine you are encouraging him and sharing how God has a plan for us. How He has provided in the past. Maybe you are planting after all…

I stood at the window and watched you this morning.
As I watched, I prayed for you. That God would give you encouragement and that He would remind you
that He loves you and is working in both our lives for our good and His glory. I prayed He would help us
remember all He has done for us in the past. I prayed for wisdom to learn the lessons He is teaching.
I prayed that I would be a good help-mate and be patient when you are discouraged. I thanked God for
you and for our many years together. He will get us through this one as well.

I stood at the window and watched you this morning.
As I said "Amen," I remembered the song, *Standing on the Promises*.
I added another prayer…that He would remind us to stand on His promises. That He promised to
never leave or forsake us. And that we need to rest in Him as our 'all in all.'

Written by: Lori Zimmerman

Endnotes

[i] Rodman, M., & Rodman, M. (2019). Flea Market. In 1142005713 859744906 M. Rodman (Ed.), *Live Life in Full Bloom* (1st ed., Vol. 2, Bloom Daily Devotional Series, p. 180). Weatherford, TX: Legacy Lane Publishing.

[ii] Tew, R. (2015, July 16). Don't wait for everything to be perfect before you decide to enjoy your life. Retrieved June 15, 2020, from s://livelifehappy.com/life-quotes/dont-wait-for-everything/

[iii] Exodus 9. (2004). In *Life application study Bible: New Living Translation* (p. 109). Wheaton, IL: Tyndale House.

[iv] John 21. (2004). In *Life application study Bible: New Living Translation* (p. 1802). Wheaton, IL: Tyndale House.

[v] Batterson, M. (2013). Find Your Voice. In *Draw the circle: The 40-day prayer challenge*.

[vi] TOP 25 QUOTES BY DAVID LIVINGSTONE (of 64): A-Z Quotes. (n.d.). Retrieved November 02, 2020, from https://www.azquotes.com/author/8949-David_Livingstone

New Living Translation

Unless otherwise indicated, all Scripture quotations are taken from the Holy Bible, New Living Translation, copyright ©

1996, 2004, 2007 by Tyndale House Foundation. Used by permission of Tyndale House Publishers, Inc., Carol Stream, Illinois 60188. All rights reserved.

Noted as NIV

THE HOLY BIBLE, NEW INTERNATIONAL VERSION®, NIV® Copyright © 1973, 1978, 1984, 2011 by Biblica, Inc.® Used by permission. All rights reserved worldwide.

Noted as NKJV

Scripture taken from the New King James Version®. Copyright © 1982 by Thomas Nelson. Used by permission. All rights reserved.

Noted as MSG

"Scripture taken from *The Message*. Copyright © 1993, 1994, 1995, 1996, 2000, 2001, 2002. Used by permission of NavPress Publishing Group."

Resources

Don't Miss Out!

Go to www.MaryRodman.com
and sign up to receive emails whenever Mary Rodman publishes a new book or posts to her blog. There's no charge and no obligation.

Coming next…

Blooming Crazy Christian Devotional Series

Tidbits of encouragement from upcoming books will be available on social media. Follow Mary as MrsMaryRodman.

Discount Purchases

- All books are discounted at: www.MaryRodman.com/Books
- ***Bloom Where You're Planted*** "This beautifully written book is a delight, filled with wonderful stories from her life and awesome applications of God's truth. It will lift you up and speak words of truth and encouragement into your life." *~Doris Swift*
- ***Live Life in Full Bloom*** "Mary's words are from her heart. I can see every story, as if I was standing there watching it happen. I laughed so hard at some of the stories because, life happens in unexpected ways." ~ TJG, Amazon
- ***Bloom Daily Devotional Journals*** An inspirational quote from each devotion in the matching devotional book. Ample space to journal your thoughts, and a Daily Gratitude section.
- ***Mary Magdalene a Woman of Resilience: 5 Lessons to Develop an Irrepressible Passion for Jesus*** Give from the heart. Serve graciously. Embrace your freedom. Live with gratitude. Witness for Jesus.
- ***Cast the First Stone be Transformed by Grace: 5 Lessons to Discover the Irrepressible Grace of Jesus*** Defining Moments. The Shame. The Judgement. Patience of Christ. Irrepressible Grace. You will enjoy these lessons based on the Adulterous Woman.

Download free Resources for your next event

- Free devotions are available to you at https://maryrodman.com/landers/book-bonuses-for-bloom-in-god-s-promises
    - ***Recipes*** A collection of devotions from *Bloom Where You're Planted* and *Live Life in Full Bloom.*
    - ***Names of God*** More devotions which focus on the different names and aspects of God. From *Bloom Where You're Planted* and *Live Life in Full Bloom.*
    - ***Blooming Crazy*** A sneak peek at the next devotional series. *Blooming Crazy Christian Devotional Series* will excite you and encourage you in this crazy life we live.

Book Mary as a Speaker-Facilitator for your weekend retreat at https://maryrodman.com/press-kit

- ***Who Are You? Discover the woman God created you to be.*** *"There are many virtuous and capable women in the world, but you surpass them all!" (Proverbs 31:29).* Mary's retreat will transform your walk with Christ as she shares her funny stories, Biblical examples, and powerful messages through these four topics.
    - ***Defining Moments*** Within minutes, the Adulterous Woman had both good and bad defining moments. The moment she was dragged into public and humiliated, and the moment Jesus said, "Go and sin no more." Mary will challenge you to see both bad and good defining moments as good when used for God's glory.
    - ***God Loves You*** God loves the woman He created—exactly like you are, with all your flaws, gifts, talents and idiosyncrasies. Biblical story: Samaritan Woman.
    - ***Who Are You?*** Mary Magdalene was possessed by seven evil spirits. Christ changed her life dramatically when He cast out the demons. She was transformed into a servant for Christ and served with a gracious heart.
    - ***Dare to Dream*** Caleb dreamed of the Promised Land for over forty years, but patiently waited for the Lord to lead the battle. Your dreams will also come into fruition when you align your dreams with God's will.
- This weekend retreat is available in multiple formats.
    - One or two day event.
    - Mary as a speaker. She will present the four talks and provide breakout questions for your small groups.
    - Mary as both the speaker and the facilitator for your event.

- Optional music by Angie Greenwood. Angie's musical talent as a worship leader and soloist is uplifting and inspirational.

Book Mary as a keynote speaker for your next event. Her topics include…

- ***Something out of Nothing*** While in a season of grief Mary discovered she could make something out of nothing which changed her outlook on life. She will help you find blessings on those most difficult days of grief.
- ***Dare to Dream*** *"What you dare to dream of, dare to do." Sarah Jane Shoaf.* Learn to follow your dreams and be motivated to accomplish them by aligning your dreams with God's will.
- ***Bloom Where You're Planted*** From a wild ride down the mountainside to the heartaches of life, Mary shares how to *BLOOM* in all aspects of your life.
- ***The Woman God Sees*** God sees you as His chosen, precious, beloved, royalty. Learn how *"the Lord delights in you." (Isaiah 62:4)* through Mary's personal stories intertwined with scripture.
- ***A Christian Farm Wife's Perspective*** As a woman who wears many hats, from farmwife to speaker and author, Mary shares her struggles as a newlywed on the farm and how they learned to build their marriage around Christ on the most stressful days.
- ***Faith, Farming or Career?*** As a farmwife, Mary shares farm statistics to increase awareness of the family farm. She incorporates how faith, farming, and her career as an author and speaker all intertwine and work together for God's glory.

- ***What is Your Legacy?*** Did you realize that long after you are gone, God answers your prayers? The greatest legacy you can leave others is in the power of your prayers.
- ***Custom Topic*** Mary enjoys Bible research and sharing some of the antics from her own life. She is open to speaking opportunities on your topic of choice. Please allow six-weeks preparation time, For more information go to https://maryrodman.com/press-kit.
- Download "**Mary's One Sheet**" containing her contact information and the basis of her beliefs.

Inspire U

Stay in touch by using our messenger's treasury of Divine inspiration, insight, and guidance. **Download and join** for free ***The Inspire U app*** for additional personal resources on your mobile device today!

More Books by Mary Rodman

Always available at www.MaryRodman.com/Books

Journal your thoughts about each devotion.
Bloom In God's Promises Journal

Did you love ***Bloom In God's Promises***?
Then you should read ***Bloom Where You're Planted***!

Through laughter, memories and even sorrow, Mary helps you see the Bright Morning Star, named Jesus. Discover her humor in the devotional, Bird Poop, as she highlights the Biblical example of Abigail and how you might handle unwelcome life circumstances.

You may also enjoy ***Live Life in Full Bloom.***

Chuckle as Mary shares her rotisserie experience at the sleep clinic, and how she was humbly reminded of the blessings in her life which she had taken for granted.

Looking for a quick, thought provoking Bible study? Check out ***The Irrepressible Disciple Series***

Mary Magdalene A Woman of Resilience

Mary Magdalene was a resilient servant of Christ and a witness of His greatness How was she able to overcome her demons to become the first witness of Christ's resurrection?

Cast the First Stone Be Transformed by Grace

The Adulterous Woman experienced every emotion as she cowered at the feet of Jesus. She is about to receive His hand of grace, but at this moment in time, she doesn't know what her future holds.

About the Author

When you BLOOM with Jesus, you become a child of God who is cultivated for your beauty. This beauty does not happen overnight, it is a gradual change within your soul, because of your relationship with Jesus.

As a Christian author & speaker, Mary's objective is to point you toward Jesus. Her words are simple, and her examples are relatable, but when Jesus touches your heart it is amazing. When you follow Him wholeheartedly, and align your dreams with God's will, the outcome is life altering.

The first goals of Mary's ministry are to offer you encouragement and inspiration. She is a "seed planter." The person who sees a glimmer of hope in the small day-to-day routines of life. Therefore, the key verse for her ministry is: "When we get together, I want to encourage you in your faith, but I also want to be encouraged by yours." (Romans 1:12).

Once the seed of hope is planted in your heart, Mary motivates you to stay in God's Word to seek wisdom, and learn about Jesus' amazing grace. "If you need wisdom, ask our generous God, and he will give it to you. He will not rebuke you for asking." (James 1:5).

Mary's prayer is that you have a personal relationship with our Redeemer. For more information of God's grace, go to https://maryrodman.com/pages/god-s-promises.

Mary resides in Radnor, Ohio with her husband, Jim. Together they enjoy farm life, hard work, vacations, family and friends. She is a farm girl who discovered her niche as a Christian author and speaker. Mary loves sharing about the Lord through both her written and spoken words. Mary's life is an open book as she shares her joys, struggles and embarrassing moments.

Mary
Rodman

About the Publisher

We love helping heart-centered, Christian-principled aspiring writers, and new authors tell your compelling stories and showcase your excellence like no other. Our publishing ministry is designed to help you whether you've already written your book, or it's still a vision or a dream.

Our Promise

You retain full control over your manuscripts, cover design, and editing options. You may publish your completed project in any or all formats available. You retain full copyright privileges to all manuscripts, cover designs, or other print materials produced while working with us. You retain the freedom to publish in all languages, globally.

Legacy Lane Publishing
www.LegacyLanePublisng.com

Mary Rodman

Mary Rodman

www.ingramcontent.com/pod-product-compliance
Lightning Source LLC
LaVergne TN
LVHW091038080826
845145LV00002B/541